The JOURNEY Home

AN OPEN INVITATION

You are invited. Annually, In the Garden Publishing will extend a personal invitation to the world to participate in The Journey Home Global Collaborative Book Project.

Each volume will feature a specific theme and a variety of guest authors. Always the central theme will be a variation of the ever-expanding knowledge that each one of us is individually a unique expression of the Divine.

It is in this recognition of your true nature that one can begin to live a more balanced life in mind, body and spirit. In a renewed state of harmony within, we transform the world without.

What is required? Truly, only a shift in perception. This perceptive shift into Conscious Awareness seems to be approaching critical mass whether or not you believe any of the hype surrounding 2012.

What has been your experience? The Journey Home, at its core, is a collection of love letters as we travel down the path of discovery. And what an amazing journey! Won't you join us?

Follow / Participate in *The Journey Home* Annual Global Collaborative Open Book Project by visiting:
www.GroundingHeavenAsEarth.com

In this Book Series:

The Journey Home: Discover Heaven on Earth
Volume 1 - 2012

The JOURNEY Home

Awakening in the Dream

VOLUME 2

2013

in the garden Publishing

a media company of
WHAT WOULD LOVE DO INT'L LTD

Copyright © 2013 In the Garden Publishing
www.IntheGardenPublishing.com

All rights reserved. No part of this publication may be reproduced in whole or in part, or transmitted in any form by any means electronic, mechanical, magnetic, and photographic including photocopying, recording or by any information storage and retrieval system without prior written permission by the publisher, except for the brief inclusions of quotations in a review. No patent liability is assumed with respect to the use of the information contained herein. Although every precaution has been taken in the preparation of this book, the publisher and author assume no responsibility for errors or omissions. Neither is any liability assumed for damages resulting from the use of the information contained herein. Note that this material is subject to change without notice.

"Answer to a Prayer" adapted from "Discovery" from HIDDEN TREASURE: UNCOVERING THE TRUTH IN YOUR LIFE STORY, Copyright © 2011 by Gangaji. Used by permission of Jeremy P. Tarcher, an imprint of Penguin Group (USA) LLC.

ISBN: 978-0-9888333-8-8

Library of Congress data available upon request.

Cover and Interior Design by Christine Horner

Published by:

IN THE GARDEN PUBLISHING
P.O. Box 752252
Dayton, OH 45475

www.IntheGardenPublishing.com
www.WhatWouldLoveDoIntl.com

CONTENTS

AN OPEN INVITATION 3
    PREFACE 9
    INTRODUCTION 11
    Chapter 1: Emma Bickley 15
      The Sun is Always Shining
    Chapter 2: Fred Davis 27
      From Desolation to Deliverance
    Chapter 3: Courtney Dukelow 43
      Love's Divine Forms
    Chapter 4: Shanti Einolander 47
      Altar of Longing
    Chapter 5: Gangaji 67
      Answer to a Prayer
    Chapter 6: Christine Horner 85
      When It's Personal
    Chapter 7: Sahaja Jaeger 95
      Bushwhacked by Grace
    Chapter 8: Amoda Maa Jeevan 105
      Untamable Fire
    Chapter 9: Scott Kiloby 117
      When Love Comes Into Form

Chapter 10: Hillary Larson 123
    The Last Place I Thought to Look

Chapter 11: Zubin R. Mathai 131
    The Mystery of Our Unfolding

Chapter 12: Sutra Ray Robinson 147
    Floored by Truth

Chapter 13: Jessica Rzeszewski 153
    The Space of One Moment

Chapter 14: Kia Scherr 165
    Forgiveness: Key to Peace, Gateway to Openness

Chapter 15: Elizabeth Schmidt-Pabst 171
    LOVE of My Life

Chapter 16: Miriam Louisa Simons 179
    what is this?

Chapter 17: Unmani 195
    Never Forgotten

Chapter 18: Enza Vita 207
    Enlightenment is Not an Experience

Chapter 19: Alison Walker 215
    A Christmas Gift

Chapter 20: Zenju Earthlyn Manuel 227
    The Way of Tenderness

PREFACE

It is an honor and a privilege to partner with Shanti Einolander, founder of OneTheMagazine, for Volume 2 of *The Journey Home*, an Annual Global Collaborative Open Book Project.

This volume would not have been possible without the loving and giving hearts of all of our contributors. Heartfelt thanks goes to: Emma, Fred, Courtney, Shanti, Gangaji, Sahaja, Amoda Maa, Scott, Hillary, Zubin, Sutra Ray, Jessica, Kia, Elizabeth, Miriam, Unmani, Enza, Alison, and Zenju.

Also, we are thankful to Penguin Group (U.S.) for the permissions necessary to reprint Gangaji's words, and to Gangaji for the many lives she has touched, as evidenced throughout the pages of this book.

The production of this book was clearly orchestrated by the Universe, guided by inspiration and a simple request that was met by a warm, "Yes, I would love to!" It is demonstrated repeatedly in our lives that life really is meant to be joyfully lived, from a place of ease, when we set aside personal agendas and allow ourselves to become the blank canvas with which the Universe can paint through.

Gangaji, Unmani, as well as many other contributors have written books which are mentioned at the end of each chapter in the author's bio. If you were moved as much as we were upon reading these stories, please feel free to reach out to the authors to express your gratitude via personal websites, e-mail, social media, and please seek out their books.

If you enjoyed this book, please let us know. We'd love to hear from you! See you next year for *The Journey Home* 2014!

Christine Horner
Publisher

INTRODUCTION

There is the possibility in every human life when for an instant the illusion of existing as a separate entity simply vanishes. A veil is lifted and somehow, miraculously, all of life is experienced as one seamless unified reality, and you recognize without a doubt that the truth of who you are is this one reality. Never again can you truly deny that not only are you intimately connected with every human heart and with all of life, at the core you are the fabric of life itself.

The world is waking up! The signs are all around. The global shift in consciousness predicted in the 80's and 90's has now become reality.

Over the last decade, scores of spiritual teachers of great clarity have arisen on the world stage to confirm an essential truth: We are One. We are not separate. Not separate from each other, not separate from God, not separate from *all that is*. Not as some kind of New Age catchphrase, but as a reality that can be intimately realized within oneself, here and now, regardless of circumstances.

Whether this inner revelation is called Truth, God, Awareness, or Supreme Love, this unified field of pure potentiality is essentially who we are at the core. We are existence itself, not bound by appearances of name and form. This is our true identity. To awaken to this truth while still in a human body brings unbounded joy, peace, freedom, and love—as well as endless opportunity to live one's life true to this most fundamental truth.

"Awakening" can have different meanings to different people and is often spoken about in different contexts. Whether it is simply the compassionate recognition that the suffering of another is not separate from your own; or a momentary glimpse that you are infinitely more vast than the mind-body-ego you've been conditioned to believe yourself to be; or a lightning bolt of liberation that leaves no lasting identification as a separate individual—all of it is pointing to the same truth: Who we are, each one of is, is the totality of being, and this totality is none other than love itself.

In an instant of grace we can experience coming Home to ourselves and to the astonishing discovery that in truth we were never anywhere other than Home. This is the great cosmic joke! The peace, the love, the spiritual understanding we having been searching for throughout time has never been anywhere other than here—closer than the breath, before the next thought—exactly as we are. All this time, our true nature has simply been veiled by the activity of the mind and the habit of looking outside ourselves for happiness. All that is required is a moment of pure openness and the curiosity to stop, to look within, and to sincerely inquire, "Who am I, really?"

In *The Journey Home, Volume 2*, you will find a compilation of essays from beautiful souls who share some aspect of their experience of awakening. Our endless gratitude goes out to all who participated in this open book project, including you, the reader. There is a great power in coming together in support of one another's awakening. Our willingness means more than we can know. When we share our experience of awakening, when we speak about what it is to live an ordinary human life consciously aware of our shared essence as One Being, it transmits the possibility of that same grace opening within the heart of another.

May the reverberations of this sharing bring peace and happiness to every reader of this book and every being in all the realms, known and unknown.

Shanti Einolander
founder/editor, OneTheMagazine

chapter 1

The Sun is Always Shining
Emma Bickley

*Shadows play around the moon at night
Yet this light remains undimmed.*

Kia Ora Reader,

I want to start by saying I love you. Why? Because I know that like me, you are doing the best you can with what you have. Different stories maybe, but inside, we are the same. I love this. It is where we are one. Where we get caught up is when we live on the outside, in how we think oneness, peace, and love should look.

Chapter 1

This is why I share my story with you. Not to talk about myself, but to talk about where we are the same, to participate in this global awakening conversation, and to discover ourselves in each other's stories. To really discover what oneness is to us in everyday life, beyond the idealized versions of the mind.

My story is not pretty, but certainly not the worst of stories. To many people I would have been considered a fairly useless human being, so this is fantastic to share. Sharing the redemption in crappy life stories can show NOTHING is wasted. All is included in the fundamental sense that it is here. Life happens in a multitude of ways. To deny this is to bring about our own downfall, individually and collectively. This is my discovery, and I offer it in support of you.

The journey has in essence been about discovering what was here all along. A long, somewhat torturous, route, yet one I am grateful for. I've always been a questioner with boundless curiosity. Innocent as a child, yet with the onset of adulthood my perception of life became much darker. The Christian religion of my childhood held safe parameters. Yet when my adolescent self discovered the shallowness of the dogma and walked away from it, Life became full of grey areas, and with this awareness came the terror of the unknown. I was a sponge for feeling the horrors of the world. I became increasingly fatalistic and nihilistic. My heart broke for the world, yet still I prayed. I knew I was going to succumb to follow my desire to use drugs to dull the pain. I felt completely useless and out of control. Yet I prayed to the god of my understanding that at some point my experiences would be of use, and that I would be of use. In a moment of prayer, I heard the words:

You do not need to follow this path to help others, but if you do, know that it will end within 10 years. You will be restored.

This revelation was true to its word. For nine and a half years I lived the life of a heroin/morphine addict. It took a few years to get in the grips of it, but I remember the moment of being fully in it. I sat on the floor with the needle in my vein and cried. I cried because I knew I could not stop, and that this addiction would possibly kill me. I forgot the promise of the revelation and surrendered to the addiction. There was no longer any feeling of choice and the desire to use opiates eclipsed all else.

It is amazing to me that I am still here. The people I was with, the situations I was in... It is amazing. Small time drug dealing and prostitution were my means of survival. Whilst working as a prostitute I was raped and nearly murdered. During this experience, I realized that whatever was happening to my body, there was something that could not be touched. I was not numb or disconnected, but fully aware as an animal is when they are trapped.

Chapter 1

The opportunity came to escape the rapist and all my instincts seized the moment.

From that moment on I started baby steps to get away from being in these situations. It took a long time. Long and painful. It was a long dark night. I kept relapsing into addiction. Finally I went on a methadone program. I hid in my room. I had counseling and explored many spiritual paths. I had many spiritual and inner experiences through exploring many different spiritual practices. I became focused on creating the better life. It had not yet occurred to inquire into the source of the "I." "I was fully attached to my ideas of who I was, and I couldn't seem to get that peace and success I so longed for. There were things in play I couldn't see. Lingering depression and anxiety, a stressed nervous system and a stubborn personality.

When I was a solo mum with beautiful twins, I became very sick and my fragile attempt at a new, better life and spiritual identity became unstuck. The terror of the unknown prevailed and all strategies proved useless. I tried hard though. I persisted at many spiritual and personal growth techniques and became quite good at some of them. Some aspects of life even improved. I experienced much less anxiety from meditation practice. My mind and emotions were clearer due to improved self-care and awareness. Yet still there was this irk, this itch that I somehow hadn't quite found "IT" yet. Where was it? I couldn't answer that. Like the moon on a cloudy night, the clarity of inner light was evasive. All I knew was that there was more to me and to life than worldly stuff and knowledge could give me.

In the ways of those who went before me, I partook of recommended practices. I chanted, drummed, and meditated in an attempt to make my inner sun rise. There were many glimpses, yet it had its own timing. I would participate in things like oneness blessings and just get annoyed. Intellectually I knew I already was love, peace, oneness, etc.

"Why do I need to do any practice to be what I am?!" I exclaimed to myself.

I walked away from all the groups, including ones I used to run, determined to give myself this chance of full unmistakable discovery. Something that was more permanent than the comings and goings of experiences. Staring out the window one day, I said to myself simply and honestly, *I need help. Nothing I do works or makes sense on a deeper level. Perhaps someone can show me what I am not getting.*

Then I carried on with my day. I checked my emails. In my inbox was an article sent to me written by a spiritual teacher named Gangaji. It was an answer to my prayer. She said that truth and peace could be discovered in everyday life, in any moment or

Chapter 1

circumstance. I didn't need to go anywhere or do anything special. This made so much sense. Her words spoke to the place in me that is the same in her. She had my attention.

Diary excerpt, 2011

It was a quiet sunny day. Numerous attempts on my part to access a Gangaji conference online brought not frustration but quiet determination. Papaji's words echoed in my ears: "Just take 30 seconds to stop and see what is here." The warm wood of the chair supported my body, my arms resting where they lay beside my laptop. "OK, this is the place and this is the time," I thought. A silent atom bomb erased the world as I knew it. The apocalypse was my own silent recognition of the truth of myself. Its grace a silent tsunami washing away everything until even the AHHHHHHHH of recognition fell into the silence of truth. The result revealed eternity and the landscape of perception turned inside out. The apocalypse revealed the simplicity of what it is staggeringly, finally, nothing at all. No Emma, just space. Thoughts, emotions, even my body, as impermanent as clouds in the sky of being.

The last few years I have received deeply from Gangaji's invitation and tested everything she says within my own life. The fruit of this is the discovery of truth. Not "the" truth or "a" truth. Just the freshness of the moment freed to be itself. Life has given the support needed every step of the way. Everything is fuel for the fire and arises moment to moment. The knowledge of this releases even the need for healing or forgiveness. Everything was as it was with my life because it couldn't be any other way. Over time, the fire of pure being devours every thought and ideology I have about how "I" think life should look. The result, a deeper compassion, peace, and truthful living.

There have been many insights and revelations, yet they all revolve around a simple truth. I cannot know myself intellectually. I can only experience a taste of the vastness of this truth and live its unfolding moment to moment. This has led to the most intimate relationship with myself and all of life I have ever experienced. It has led to just simply being alive and trusting beyond trust. It is easy to invalidate and mistrust your own experience by comparing yourself with others:

"Others have it worse than me; I shouldn't feel this way." "Someone else is more talented, attractive, intelligent, so I shouldn't bother doing what I would really like to." And the classic, "I or they should be doing better than I/they am/are."

This then denies us the opportunity to see what our own lives are showing us. For me, denying my own experience allowed depression to flourish and then to devastate my 20's. Meeting life as it stands allows for deepening insight, bringing deep healing and relief. This relief supports me to meet my life circumstances,

Chapter 1

emotions, mind, body, life as it is. The issues of depression and anxiety have resolved themselves through firstly accepting they were here. The peace of acceptance allows clarity of thought and action. Discovering the eternal support of my own being reveals when it is appropriate to seek outside support.

I am still an inquisitive, questioning being, yet it is a natural curiosity and is not troubling. Some things have answers, some things don't. I don't know what will happen tomorrow, same as everyone. The things I am passionate about and love are the same—truth, music, people, and the earth. In a way, passion is clearer because I don't get hung up on stuff the way I used to. I don't do the spiritual practices that I used to, simply because the need for them has passed. It is a supremely quiet and ordinary life. I recently successfully finished treatment for hepatitis C. I am a mum, so need to financially support our lives. To this end I am looking to finish my degree in social work because this is an area that interests me. Pretty ordinary chop wood/carry water stuff. Yet throughout it is an ongoing amazement and appreciation that was not here before when I was trying to make life better. Each moment is special in its own simple merit, needing no adornment of drugs or ritual to shine. It was easy to miss this when following the antics of thought.

The Sun is Always Shining

The simplicity of nature is a beautiful teacher. One that I love to spend time with. Sitting in shared silence, the most profound wisdom is shared freely. Sunrise has become my favorite time of day and source of inspiration. I love the different textures and flavors revealed by different seasons and weathers. Some sunrises are forged in the deep silent cold of winters. The crispness of the air lending each color distinctive notes of clarity and brilliance. The view can catch you like the cold in your throat revealing wintery beauty, as the colors light up frozen hill and vale. Other sunrises flower within benevolent summers. The light in the sky growing as an opulent tropical flower, matching the raucous call of the thousands of birds who add to the display. Here one might be found lying in the sand, warmed by earth and sky to then leap and race into the orange foam.

Watching people open to themselves as life as it is in that moment is a glorious sunrise I am in awe of. To share in the moment as another soul lights up with their inner fire, brings me to bended knee. Our awakenings are as varied as the many life forms here on earth. Some awakenings are forged in deep cold winters of a life. The awakening sun within them brings deep release of frozen lakes of emotion. Summer awakenings bring a deeper freedom that, even while life is great, there is deeper force within that satisfies like no summer can.

Chapter 1

The truth is that the sun is always shining. In deep winters, the sun is shining. On stormy days, the sun is shining. Wherever we are, in whatever kinds of seasons and weathers, the sun is shining. That is what it does and is here to do.

Sometimes I meet a person who is in a dark gloomy season, just as I once was. Whilst sunrise is not apparently here, still the sun is shining and sunrise will come. It has to, especially if it is ardently sought after. Seasons pass, winter gives way to warmth, warmth gives way to cold, and all the while the sun shines. For me, the depths of the darkness revealed such beauty that when the sun rose I laughed and laughed. I laughed because I saw the sun shining in the dark, and I knew it had always been shining.

Once I had a dream that I was a part of a tribe. We lived, slept, and gave birth amidst snowdrifts in the highest mountain peaks. It was a harsh yet deeply silent and peaceful existence, carved out in the deepest cold, yet also the most brilliant, clear sunlight, as the harshness of the mountains revealed the most stunning vistas. One day people from the lower lands came and asked me to join them at a gathering to share of our lives. People came and shared of the many corners of their worlds. No one was trying to be another. We were all honored as a unique strand in the tapestry of life on earth, no one indivisible from the whole.

The Sun is Always Shining

This story I have shared is such a strand. This magazine, and any other gathering of sharing like this, is a beautiful space to honor the many colors of our lives, and the truth discovered in the core of each of our circumstances. For me this has meant that nothing has changed, yet everything has changed. This center of peace is not dependent upon anything. Indeed it doesn't even exist. Finally, no matter what the weather, the sun is always shining. Such a secret joy this knowledge. Yet one that must be shared. It catches me again and again and again, leaving me giggling. It is infectious. I hope you catch it, even though you already have it.

Peace is...

To all who become lost, I celebrate and say:
"To lose oneself is the only way to find
That, which you did not know you were looking for."

Om Mani Padme Om—the jewel in the lotus. Your own dear self.

If my sharing has moved you in some way that you want to say hi, e-mail me: heartsharingcircle@gmail.com

Arohanui,

Emma

© 2013 Emma Bickley

Chapter 1

Emma Bickley lives in Auckland New Zealand with her family. She is completing her Bachelor of Social Work. Also she writes poetry and loves to create events around music and sharing the experience of being human. You can find her on Facebook or e-mail her at: heartsharingcircle@gmail.com

chapter 2

From Desolation to Deliverance

Fred Davis

It was early autumn of 1998 when I found myself living in Mount Tabor City Park in Portland, Oregon. Yes, I was *living* there, in a park, in the bushes, scared and hungry, with blisters on my feet the size of the palm of your hand. When you're homeless, the police don't even *want* to arrest you. You're not worth the trouble. So they just nudge you along, keeping you moving, moving, always moving. Not on *my beat*, buddy.

I had sold my sleeping bag to buy a couple of bottles, and then I'd caught some kind of lung infection. My voice sounded like rocks grinding against each other. I wished I would die, but I

Chapter 2

noticed I didn't. That's the funny thing about alcoholism; it kills you if and when *it* wants to, not when *you* want it to. As the booze ran out and I began to have to face reality, I couldn't help but look back to a decade before.

In 1988 I had been living in the suburbs of Columbia, South Carolina. I owned an enormously successful comic, gaming, and science fiction shop. I had a great wife, a nice house, four nice cars, and according to my lawyer and accountant, I had a fine future ahead of me. All I had to do was not screw it up. That's a difficult thing for a practicing alcoholic to avoid. I had not the first clue on how to handle success, because it wasn't anything I was particularly familiar with. I was a crazy man with money.

But let's drop back a little further. When I used to tell my story in public I got to where I told it backwards, just to make sure I kept both me and the audience awake. I guess I'm doing that here as well.

In 1982 I woke up—that's always what it felt like at the end of a long run of drunkenness and active insanity—to find myself getting bed and board in the G. Werber Bryan Psychiatric Hospital in Columbia. This was a place where the doors were locked, I wasn't issued a key, and I wasn't allowed to play with anything sharp. I did get all the crayons I wanted.

From Desolation to Deliverance

This was my second visit to the same institution. I'd been there a year before and hadn't learned a damn thing. I was not big on learning; I was big on repeating. I know now that it was all part of a vast pattern, but at that time I'm afraid I was unable to bring the "light of consciousness" to bear on my wanton lifestyle. This second time around, however, a voice went off in my head as I sat in the dayroom drawing with my crayons. From out of nowhere and clear as a bell it said, "You should study Zen."

It would not have been any more ridiculous if the voice had said, "You should grow horns," or "You should take a look at quantum physics." Here is what I knew about Buddhism:

I had been out to Boulder and visited Chogyam Trungpa's Naropa Institute, which is now a university. It certainly wasn't then. This was 1976, and it was a wonderful madhouse with lots of serious Buddhists, artists, chakra workers, Rolfers and all kinds of folks who were misbehaving just badly enough to make things really interesting. However, I certainly wasn't there for Buddhism and found it an annoying distraction to my chief task. I was a drunken, romantic poet, straight (in my mind) out of Jack Kerouac's *On the Road,* and I was hunting down Allen Ginsberg at the Jack Kerouac School of Disembodied Poetics. I found him, too, along with Peter Orlovsky, Gregory Corso, and a bunch of other Beats I'd read about. Heady stuff. Great for drinking stories.

Chapter 2

I happily invaded a house that the university owned and rented out to students. They generously housed me and kindly fed me, and in return I drank all their wine (several gallon jugs of it that I found in the basement where I slept in the bed Corso had recently abandoned). On my first night there at a party at Ginsberg's, I met a lot of the characters who were in *On the Road,* and I thought I'd died and gone to heaven.

What I'm telling you is that here I was, in the very *heart* of a slowly awakening America, and I didn't want *any* of it. Allen wanted to talk about sitting practice, and I wanted to talk about *Howl,* his wildly controversial literary bombshell. Fortunately, all of us wanted to drink, so I fit right in for a day or two. It was in the Naropa house that I made my first acquaintance with meditation cushions. I thought they made fine drinking stools, and if you fell off of them, you didn't have far to fall, which was great.

This all took place about six years before I woke up in the psychiatric hospital and heard the voice in my head saying, "You should study Zen." Prior to that strange moment in the asylum, that time in Colorado had represented the sum total of my knowledge—and interest—in things Buddhist or awakened, and as I sat in Bryan Psychiatric, I was—guess what—homeless and penniless. I had just come out of the Arizona desert where I had *also* nearly died. This was the only reason I paid any attention to that voice at all. If I'd had any other idea at all, I'm sure I wouldn't be writing this today. But I *didn't* have any other idea. What I did have was a voice in my head that spoke clearly and authoritatively and had a suggestion. So, to my amazement, when I was loosed from the institution—after promising not to kill myself *right away* and thus cast dispersions on their care—I took my voice's suggestion.

This was the beginning of an off and on, up and down spiritual journey that was to last twenty-five years. Since there was no Zen in my town, I tried to join the Tibetans in my town, but soon discovered I wasn't a joiner. If I wasn't going to be made Dalai Lama, I didn't need them, though they thankfully taught me how to meditate properly. Years later I tried to join the Zen crew in Portland, but once again, if there was no room for Fred Davis-Roshi, I just couldn't be bothered.

So I studied and practiced independently, diligently, even relentlessly (when I studied and practiced). Then I started making money and all that quickly went away. However, once I drank my way out of all that money, I once again found the idea of spirituality appealing. It was a way for me to win. I thought if I could just get enlightened, hopefully with a bunch of followers (mostly women would be fine), then I could sort of feel like my waste of a fine slice of the American Dream had all been a clever plan. Of course it was all just madness.

Chapter 2

In Portland, in 1992, I had my first real glimpse of my true nature. Sadly, I was deep in my cups at the time, and ego simply lapped that up and christened me, "special." Understand, I was a drunken *car salesman,* but I nonetheless shaved my head, started wearing all black, and ran my poor wife off for a while. I eventually became functional again—for a practicing alcoholic, mind you—but that single night of freedom haunted me and taunted me like Dickens' Christmas ghosts. I just couldn't let go of it. It gnawed and gnawed at me, but reality just couldn't quite get through the alcoholism and unveil itself again. Until it did, of course. But I'm getting ahead of myself again.

I got out of that park by powering my way through a couple of bureaucrats who were used to saying no to people who had better odds of recovery but less personal drive than I had. They told me to leave the crisis hospital and I said no. I kept saying no until they had a homeless shelter come pick me up and take me to the bed I'd been told didn't exist. I bow to the city of Portland for their crisis, detox, shelter, and recovery programs. That saved my life, plain and simple. Thank you very much.

It took me another two years to get sober, but the park was my bottom. Not a week goes by that I don't mention it, and it's been almost fifteen years since I was there. For a while I went back and forth between Twelve Step recovery and drunkenness until I once again hit a very bleak spot, and the park rose up in my vision. I knew I couldn't go there again. I couldn't take that level of misery anymore. I knew I had to quit drinking, and I knew I couldn't do it myself. So I turned myself in to the recovery people, fully surrendered—*to my alcoholism only*—at long last.

I was one of those guys who jumps into recovery with both feet. I hit the ground running and I didn't stop moving for more than a decade. I got very involved in working the steps. I worked them poorly, as I see it now, but enthusiastically. I used to tell people that apparently God paid more attention to *intent* that she did form. I saw a lot of people do the steps perfectly who never got through them and ended up in the ditch again. More than anything on earth, I wanted to stay out of the ditch. Frankly, I didn't want to stop drinking. Not for a minute. But I wanted a life again, and I wanted to stay out of the park, and if surrendering to formal recovery was what it took for me to stay sober, so be it. I personally, and a ton of guys I worked with for the next eleven years, benefited from that moment of clarity. Getting sober was the smartest decision I *never* made. Call it grace. There's nothing else to call it.

I cut no corners. I would tell guys I worked with, "All I can do is tell you how I did it, and I did it the hard way; I did it *their* way." And that's the truth. I was cookie cutter recovery, straight out of the book. And it worked! I got sober, and my life began to stabilize.

Chapter 2

To this day, thirteen years later, I've never regained really solid financial footing. I never made it a priority. I made getting and staying sober a priority for a while, and then I made stretching the bounds of my spiritual experience a priority, and there just wasn't time or opportunity for a whole lot else. I was 47 years old when I got sober, a guy with a heavily checkered past, so it made sense to make my demands minimal.

When I was 18 months sober I let myself read my first Zen book in a long time. It took about three minutes for me to see where I was headed: a Non-dual path of recovery. I learned to transfer Non-dual teachings into recovery-speak so that no one would be offended. When I got to the rooms of recovery, all I wanted was to get sober. Now that I was sober, all I wanted was enlightenment. I went at it as relentlessly as I went after sobriety.

In 2002, I discovered Eckhart Tolle, and that changed everything. I read, listened, watched, and dreamed Eckhart Tolle for the next two years. And it's a damn good thing I did, because I was arrested in 2004 for having been a less-than-wonderful guy back in my drinking days. Some Ninth Step work, which is where we make amends for our wrongs, backfired on me. I spent the next two years in fear of prison as I waited for my trial. I didn't go to prison, but I did land in an ugly life situation, and I wanted to die. But my then-girlfriend, now-wife's business partner had shot himself in the head in 2002, and I had helped her clean up the detritus of his life and death. It was very ugly, and took a real toll on her, and there was no way on earth I was going to commit unblessed suicide on her. She promised she would bless it if things didn't work out, but asked me to please give life a chance. Much to my chagrin, I did.

So, I felt like I couldn't live, but I clearly couldn't die either. I was caught in a vise. I didn't see it coming, but this *viceness* is a perfect set-up for a spontaneous awakening, should one feel like making a visitation, so to speak. In September 2006, while sitting in my living room in total life delusion and misery, that "visitation" arrived for a second time, fourteen years after the first glimpse. This was more than a glimpse; a lot more. I came to know my true nature. In conventional spiritual language, I "woke up."

It was quite an awakening—it felt like it took the top of my head off. I moved from misery to bliss in the blink of an eye. Suddenly, I *knew*. I knew who I was and I knew that everything was *just fine,* even the beat up little human unit I'd thought myself to be, but which I was now *looking at* from slightly behind and above. I saw clearly that "Fred" was just a story, just a label attached to an automated pattern. And since Fred was empty, so were all of his deep fears and dark concerns. It was all *empty,* every bit of it. When seen from awareness itself, all was well in the world, all was *unimaginably* fine in the world of dreams and drama.

Chapter 2

Before I go any further here, let me say that what I am describing here is a *spiritual experience.* This experience was the sideshow, not the awakening. Experiences of this magnitude are fairly rare, I think, and if you don't have one you'll probably be better off. There is *no intrinsic connection* between this spiritual experience and enlightenment. As beautiful and profound as these experiences can be, they are very likely to serve chiefly as *distractions.* We get so caught up in the candy that *accompanied* awakening that we *overlook* awakening itself.

Awakening can be very subtle, or very sharp, as it was in my case, or anywhere in between. Realization itself is *not* about visions, or an LSD-like experience, or feeling vast and blissful. That's the candy. It's great, and I'm all for a hot and spicy spiritual experience, but it is *completely* unnecessary. I've had dozens of people wake up while talking to me, and very few of them have had an explosive experience. Often there are tears and laughter, and once in a while there's a big bang, but just as often there is a simple "Oh." Or maybe an "Oh, wow." And this is sometimes followed by, *"Oh my God!"* It's a lot of fun to be a part of these awakenings; every one of them is different, and every one of them is wonderful.

Realization came, at least for me, in the way of an initial *download,* so to speak, followed by a series of downloads. I actually didn't get all that many direct *answers,* but the knowledge I *did* get caused nearly all of my questions to dissipate. Here's another example of that.

I once sat down to lunch with a woman I thought was a nearly hopeless case. From what she'd told me in the first few minutes of our meeting, in my mind she wasn't even on the *planet* where awakening *could* happen. But she'd gone to a lot of trouble to meet with me, so with a heavy heart and all the enthusiasm I could muster, I gave her my absolute best shot.

An hour into our conversation she grabbed my hand and burst into tears. She just held my hand, looked up at me, and cried like a baby. She *knew,* and I knew she knew. "Welcome home," I told her as she cried across the table from me. She then proceeded to spend the next hour sounding like someone who'd been awake for *years.* Her whole use of language shifted as understanding dawned. She sounded like a *spiritual teacher.* Instantly. It was the most amazing, radical shift I'd ever seen.

In my own experience, insight followed insight, as I came to see more and more over the course of several days. When we discover that we are the vastness, the awake space that is already everywhere, and already awake, it is startling. It's *always* a surprise. During this same time period, however, ego was doing a rapid rebuild. Yes, it happens. In fact, in my experience as a teacher, it almost *always* happens. And then the brightness begins to fade. I found myself no

Chapter 2

longer operating from present realization, but from *memory* of a *former* realization. This is the well-trodden path, but I didn't know it at the time. We call this phenomenon "oscillation."

Yet despite a lot of back and forth oscillation for a few years, I never could truly unsee what I'd seen; although the "overwhelming" quality of realization has now, thankfully, gone away. Now, everything is just sort of *steady*. Take it from me, steady is much, much better than the bliss candy that often accompanies an awakening. You don't need it, and you're probably better off if you don't get it. A nice, quiet "aha!" is much easier to deal with, and a good deal less distracting.

I went through the cycling of "I-got-it, I-lost-it" for 3 1/2 years, until the spring of 2010, when I spent 45 minutes on the phone one evening with Scott Kiloby. He easily pulled me out of that unsteady motion, and into stability with some simple inquiry. Later he helped me orient within this brighter awakeness through continued pointers and dialoguing. I learned that lesson well. It's what I do for others now. I've come full circle.

So I had reached steady-ness, but I still wasn't really *clear*. In the same way that I invaded the Naropa house in Boulder, I invaded Greg Goode's email account. I'd read his book *Standing as Awareness* and was completely blown away by it. He was a friend of Scott's, so I introduced myself, and then regularly hijacked his attention for the next year or so. What a gentleman! I hounded him with countless emails, always presenting my highest view only to have him dismiss *it* without dismissing *me*. That's an art, and he's got it in spades.

I also spent a year or so in online satsangs with Rupert Spira. There was just a small group of us early on, so that I could really engage Rupert in a one-on-one, very meaningful and illuminating way. There just aren't a whole lot of people who are clearer than the folks who so kindly helped me. It would have been cruel to unload this much insanity and arrogance on just one man, so I'm glad the universe mercifully did it the way it did. When I started the website *Awakening Clarity* in the summer of 2011, I left the recovery world, because I knew I could no longer serve two masters. Insofar as the website goes, I had no idea what I was doing. But one of the things I had unknowingly done was open up a way for me to write out my junk. I freely aired my ongoing awakening, along with my missteps and my arrogance. It was great; I recommend it. I also soon found myself addressing a growing worldwide audience, which really made me think and test whatever I put down. "Do you really know this for yourself?" And "Is it really true for you?" were the two questions I constantly entertained. They are great questions to ask yourself as you go along. Forget answers. Go for questions. It's inquiry that frees us.

Chapter 2

If we don't impede it, spiritual awaking is an organic thing, ever-changing as we become clearer and clearer. The goal is not to transcend relativity, but to embrace it. I am not *exclusively* this little man who's typing this, but I *am* that little man. I am not *exclusively* the vastness, but I am *also* the vastness. I am *both*. I am the *whole* thing, the *one* thing—*this* thing. And you can say the same. Everyone can, whether they are clear, or cloudy.

Today, I write about Non-duality and I teach via Skype, or through my website, or wherever. Who could guess or dream of such a turnabout? From a destitute guy dying in the bushes of a city park to having the opportunity to facilitate and counsel people all over the world? It's almost inconceivable. You have to ask yourself, *What were the odds this would happen?* One hundred percent. It *had* to happen, because it happened. There is no alternative to *what is,* no parallel universes where woulda-coulda-shoulda rule. There is just This. *THIS* that is right here, right now, and This is *enough.*

I can't write any more without launching into self-promotion. That's something this unit does, and I have to keep an eye on it. Back in my days in recovery, some people would talk about being too nervous to tell their drunkalogue-and-redemption story in a public meeting of their peers. The only thing that ever made *me* nervous was the idea that somebody might get to the microphone before *I* did. This unit is a ham. It's apt to misbehave.

So I'll end here . . .

© 2013 Fred Davis

———————

Fred Davis is the creator and editor of the non-dual website, "Awakening Clarity Now." His online teaching, which has reached four continents, specializes in a method of Direct Pointing that encourages *immediate* recognition of our shared true nature. Fred is the author of two books: *The Book of Undoing: Direct Pointing to Non-dual Awareness,* and *Beyond Recovery: Non-duality and the Twelve Steps.* He can be reached through his website: www.awakeningclaritynow.com or his blog: www.awakening-clarity.blogspot.com

chapter 3

Love's Divine Forms

Courtney Dukelow

I remember it as if it were yesterday...

I was in church and my twin sister and I were practicing the song for the church performance. It was a song about the 10 commandments, and I remember it to this day:

"Number One, we have just begun; God should be first in your life. Number two, the idol rule; dah, dah, dah dah..."

When the time came to sing our one line in the song, I felt much passion and enthusiasm in my heart. When we got up to sing, this OVERWHELMING LOVE, overcame me in the deepest way. It

Chapter 3

expanded out of my heart and felt like it filled every cell of my being before extending out into the entire space. It was a love that I knew included absolutely everything, even the parts of myself that weren't so pure, parts that could get upset with my sisters or stray from the commandments. Somehow, I knew it was God's gift to me that I should hold secretly and closely in my heart and not share with any of my family. I had an experience of God that day, and I knew that God was this amazing Love that would be with me at all times.

Of course, what I didn't realize then, because of my religious conditioning at the time, was that *I am this Love*. It wasn't until 14 years later, when I met Gangaji, that this same love revealed itself in my heart and *as* my heart and ALL HEARTS. What an absolutely amazing homecoming to this timeless truth of Perfect Love.

In my experience, awakening to this love is not like a one-time realization and then that is "it." How I experience it, is that there is an ageless, timeless, and ever-present reality of Being, and then there is my human embodiment of Beingness that is deepened through meeting my own life challenges, conditioning, and circumstances.

Four years ago, I was living in Brazil and experiencing a period of personal challenge. I was meeting a lot of grief, fear, and pain that was somehow blocking my desire to embrace and embody my feminine nature in a deeper way. In facing into this, something began to open up in me. Instead of that feminine energy being directed out towards another, it opened within to this amazing, vast connection and deep realization of oneness with the Earth.

I had always experienced the amazing aliveness of the Earth, but what occurred during that time was also a realization that *she is a cosmic living being whose essence is this mystery of Love.* Her essence fills my being as I walk and touch and sit near the trees, rivers, lakes, and oceans. The magic of this intimacy touches me in ways that are like having a profound lover. The beauty of radiant love is so alive when I am in nature. There is joy in having a separate form, and in the intimacy of this meeting, the oneness reveals itself in truly sublime ways. My eyes dance in delight with the beauty of this love shining back through all forms and takes my attention to the source of my being that sees through these eyes. Loves delightful play of love loving love in all of its myriad of forms.

© 2013 Courtney Dukelow

Courtney Dukelow lives in Ashland, Oregon, where she offers energy healing, intuitive counseling, and somatic based bodywork in person and over the phone. She also leads retreats and loves to facilitate ancient indigenous ceremonies to support a deeper and

Chapter 3

more intimate connection with Mother Earth and all of life. She can be reached through her website at: www.courtneydukelow.com

chapter 4

Altar of Longing
Shanti Einolander

It's amazing, isn't it, how many lifetimes can be lived in just one? What I see looking back is something akin to a sailboat tacking madly to and fro across myriad oceans, cleaning up the karmic flotsam and jetsam of a hundred thousand lifetimes; as though we really are on the liminal threshold of a new age in consciousness and I'd better hurry up and find out the truth of myself. What I also see looking back is a lifetime constellated around the emotion of longing, a deep, incessant hunger to acquire or experience an elusive *something*.

Chapter 4

What was really wanted, I could never quite put my finger on, not in name or form, neither on the inside nor apparent outside. However, I just kept projecting this sense of longing onto whatever was my next best idea of what might satiate its endless maw.

One day the longing would reveal itself as holy desire. But in the meantime, it had a voracious appetite that shepherded this mind and body through a full spectrum of twists and turns, sometimes wonderful, often painful, certainly never boring, as it looked everywhere for an answer to itself.

Like an itch that couldn't quite be scratched, desire fueled the wild, nature-loving spirit of my youth. At times it would bunch up around itself in a big dark knot, morphing into a straitjacket of pain and grief and an immense sense of loss. I didn't understand why I felt this kind of generic emotional pain, but it served to stoke the fire even higher in a heart that ultimately longed to know its own greatness.

I yearned for something grand, something truly magnificent, something huge and real and true to take hold of this life. Whenever immersed in the hugeness of nature, the pain of the longing would disappear. Other than that, it was busy attaching itself to whatever appeared to be the next best concept, person, or object of desire that might ease its restless nature.

Of course now I know that what I wanted was freedom. Real freedom. True freedom. A life in which the mind did not play prison warden and the heart was set free.

Some pretty rough things happened in my childhood. I was jolted from my eight-year-old mantle of joy and innocence by the angst of my parent's violent arguments and subsequent divorce. My father's complete withdrawal from my life broke my little heart. I worshipped him, he was my god, and his departure was an abrupt shock.

On the heels of that was the sexual molestation perpetrated by my father's best friend, the man next door, a man I'd loved and called "Uncle" all my life.

Then there was the secret of my grandfather's alcoholism, an energy that at times seemed to suck up all the family's psychic space.

Out of this perfect storm, a longing was born, and an unconscious desire to try to find some relief from an intensity of emotion I was way too young to navigate.

At the age of eleven, I began smoking pot. Then at the tender age of fourteen, I discovered LSD. Over the course of the next couple years I "tripped" as much as I could get away with. Were these sacred substances planting seeds that would one day sprout into spiritual opening? Probably. Mostly at the time they were a distraction that attempted to fill my desire to be swept away by something greater than myself.

Also at fourteen, I got my very first taste of alcohol, which to my traumatized neurology was like nectar from the gods. Absolute heaven! Or so I thought for many years. Eventually it would manifest as my own dance with alcoholism that would not find sobriety for seventeen straight years of drinking nearly every day.

Yet despite the crazy avenues this force of misplaced longing was leading me down, somehow, by some mysterious grace, a window of reprieve opened up at the ages of 15-17. Seemingly out of nowhere, I became enveloped in an extraordinary sense of inner peace. Maybe it did have something to do with that LSD after all... but, oh, what a mystery of grace! Obviously, a miraculous departure from the usual angst associated with adolescence.

During that time, my mother, my stepfather, and I had moved into a home on the San Joaquin River, just outside of Fresno, California. On the river I developed into a young hippie and devotee of nature. Since I was a bit too young to join the explosion of consciousness happening in San Francisco in the late sixties/early seventies, I decided to create a revolution of my own. To my mother's distress I insisted that I would eat only the wild plants that grew along the river, just as the American Indians had. I let the hair grow out on my legs and under my arms. I wore hiking boots with long peasant skirts and I refused to wear a bra. Most importantly during those two years, I felt deeply in touch with my soul.

When on one of my long paddles around the river or alone in my room, I was filled to the brim with peace and well-being. I felt rooted in my soul. From this place of peace, the longing that had typically felt like a pain in my heart began to take an unexpected turn. It turned itself toward God. I began to read every spiritual book I could get my 15-year-old hands on.

At first I read books by a Christian street minister. I fell in love with Christ and hung pictures of Mary and Jesus around my room. I began to have fantasies of one day preaching on the street corners, shouting out my spiritual passion and showering the people with the goodness of God. I spent a very brief time in the Christian Church, where I was tempted to go up to the altar with the others and "give my life to Christ," yet fear held me back. What did it mean to give one's life to God? I knew I wanted that, but where did the Church come into it? Something felt off. I wasn't conscious of it at the time, but it was my first grappling with the possibility of surrender and the associated fear of losing control. I left the Church and stopped carrying my Bible around school.

Shortly thereafter I discovered Herman Hesse's *Siddhartha,* and I read that book numerous times. Oh how I loved the tale of the

Chapter 4

Buddha! Somehow the way of the wandering sadhu, the path of solitary inner contemplation, made more sense to me.

Next I got my hands on a series of novels written by a Tibetan author, Lopsang Rampa, who spun tales of the lives of young monks in the monasteries of Tibet. I couldn't get enough of those books. Alone in my room, I would cry and grieve for not having been born a male in Tibet, free to live a life of devotion. As is the way with all spiritual seeking, I never questioned the conditioned belief that God or enlightenment were to be found somewhere "out there" through the right teachings or circumstances that could point me back "in here" to where I already was. I'll never forget the day, decades later, when I finally got the joke, and the deep purifying laughter that spilled forth as the complication of a million lifetimes of searching fell away.

At the age of sixteen, I found Ram Dass' *Be Here Now,* and it became my new Bible. I especially loved his account of meeting his guru, Neem Karoli Baba. He wrote of the experience of looking into his master's eyes and feeling stripped naked to the core. He told of what it was like to be absolutely and completely *seen* by someone. Oh how longed for that experience! I decided that when I grew up I was going to find a teacher and have that same experience. And the universe, being the benevolent entity that it is, would one day manifest exactly that.

Altar of Longing

By some miracle I talked my mother into allowing me to attend an experimental high school for my senior year. This was on the condition that I find a way to fund my enrollment, which I managed to do by working hard at any job I could find. These types of "free schools," as they were termed, were springing up around the country. Mine was called Ananda. There I was encouraged to pursue whatever studies interested me, and a strong will blossomed to "follow my bliss," while simultaneously developing an aptitude for self-education.

Just as had happened with Siddhartha, society and emerging hormones eventually snatched me out of those years of inner communion and thrust me back into the illusion that the answer to my inner hunger would be found somewhere in the world, most especially in having to do with those hormones.

At seventeen, I experienced my first real lover. Surely that was the answer to the longing! Yet on the heels of sexual exploration with a beloved boyfriend much older than I, came the newfound revelation that I was actually more drawn to my best girlfriend. Hmm... I had not anticipated that one. Hadn't had a clue. Yet there it was, undeniably.

In the early seventies, homosexuality, especially in a young person, needed to be kept under wraps, if for no other reason than for one's safety, and so finding myself gay in a largely homophobic,

Chapter 4

central-California-redneck-Christian culture added yet another layer to the family shame of divorce and alcoholism. Instead of quenching the longing, the discovery of my newfound sexuality only added more fuel to the fire. How was I going to navigate my way through this new desire that had no real freedom to express itself?

I think this is when I first became consciously aware of the desire for freedom—freedom to love whomever I wanted, freedom from my growing pain and confusion, freedom that would liberate my spirit. The only outlet at that time was the dark and cheaply glitzy gay discos of central California, for which I had managed to obtain a fake ID at the age of 18. What a bleak environment in which to discover healthy relationship! Mostly what that time in the bars did was cultivate an innate talent as a pool hustler and solidify a dependence on alcohol and drugs.

As I entered my twenties, the longing got channeled into a mad love for the ocean and the intense athletic freedom of working as a scuba diving instructor and boat captain in the Hawaiian Islands. Looking back it's not hard to see how this inner ocean of longing, this yearning to find alignment with something great and real and true, had met its match in the sea.

At 23, I crossed the Pacific from Molokai to Oregon in a small sailboat with three other bright souls. In the unfolding of that 23-day crossing, I merged completely with the purity and simplicity of

Altar of Longing

wind, sun, moon, clouds, water, sunset, and sunrise. I especially fell in love with the huge albatross of the open sea—absolute power and freedom in form—and tasted once again a conscious connection to myself as a spiritual being.

Over the next 15 years I basically lived in a wetsuit and took thousands of people under the ocean, day and night, beginner and experienced, young and old. I lived and breathed and immersed myself in a great love for the sea and the sport of diving. I thrilled at helping others meet their fears and surrender to the unknown as I nurtured them into the experience of trusting, letting go, and breathing underwater.

And through all those years my addiction to alcohol continued to deepen. Luckily, I was never a falling-down drunk or a blackout drinker, but I did manage to down more than a few every evening and all day on the weekends. It seemed perfectly natural at the time. Why wouldn't a vital, young twenty-something want to have a few drinks and watch the sunset after a hard day's work on the boat or the beach? Of course I wasn't yet seeing the bottomless pit of addiction I was digging myself into.

Finally, at the age of 35, after several years of soul-wrenching back and forth, in and out of AA, I managed to find solid ground in sobriety and freedom from the demon of addiction that had attached itself to every member of my family. It was a huge turning of the tide in my life, and it came about from meeting a drunken Irish-Catholic priest.

Dear Father Patrick, with his bloodshot eyes and big rosacea nose and his can of vodka-laced Coca-Cola by his side every minute of the day and night. Something about his condition felt so sad to me, a man of God whose life and spirit were being wasted away by alcoholism. This particular mirror of myself was too close to the bone. I knew I had to surrender to sobriety once and for all, and through the grace of God I was finally able to stop the insanity. Thank you Father Patrick. I will always be grateful.

The truth is that all the while this great longing had been seeking name and form through the alcohol and the partying, the quest for relationship and the crazy, adrenaline-pumping push-it-to-the-limits deep diving, a spiritual connection to the longing had remained a glowing ember in the cave of my heart. For years it had been waiting patiently, and that authentic sense of God and self that I had experienced in those innocent teenage years was about to reawaken full force.

After living through Hurricane Iniki on Kauai in 1992, I felt it was time to finally leave Hawaii. Over the previous several years I had supplemented my diving income by acquiring a Hawaii State massage license, and I decided to move to Harbin Hot Springs in California to work as a full time massage therapist.

Altar of Longing

Over the next couple years I would also travel the Northwest and British Columbia in search of "home." Once again, I'd become fixated on finding the perfect piece of land or meeting the love of my life or both. After each foray I would return to Harbin more lost, empty, and depressed than I'd ever been. I'd finally hit bottom. I was ready to give up the search.

By that time I'd been practicing Tibetan Buddhism for nearly three years, and I decided to move back to Maui and enter the Buddhist retreat center on the eastern shore in Huelo, under the wise tutelage of the delightful Lama Tenzin. I would devote my life to spiritual practice and to becoming a Buddhist nun. I had become completely (blessedly) disillusioned with the possibility of finding any real happiness through relationship, or the right piece of land, or a satisfying career. I was finished with searching for myself in worldly endeavors. To find God, to realize enlightenment, to know my true nature, was what I wanted now more than anything, and I would devote my life to that.

Shortly after making that decision, I walked into the theatre at Harbin Hot Springs to attend the Sunday afternoon video showing reserved for spiritual teachers and teachings. On the schedule that day was an American teacher named Gangaji, whom I'd been hearing about from a number of the residents. I was curious. I was

Chapter 4

open. Yet I could never have imagined the life-altering arrow that was about to pierce my mind and heart.

As I walked into the theatre that Sunday, the video was already underway. In the moment of first seeing Gangaji's image on the screen and taking in the sound of her unusually resonant voice, something hit me full force in the center of my being. She looked so familiar. How did I know her? I tried to take in her words, the meaning of which I didn't really understand; yet at the same time I did. I recognized that she was speaking "truth," but I'd never heard anyone speak like that so directly, so openly. In my mind the same thought kept circulating: *That's me on that video. It doesn't make any sense, but somehow she is me.* And I wasn't talking about looks or personality or ways of expression. I walked back to my camper that evening in a state of wonderment and a feeling of unlimited possibility.

Soon it was time to leave for Maui and the Buddhist retreat center. My plan was to stay in seclusion at the retreat center until I had completed the four preliminary practices of Tibetan Buddhism, which I figured would take up to a year or longer. I'd seen a flyer posted of Gangaji's schedule, and synchronistically she was on her way to Maui at the same time I was. *Wonderful!* I thought. *I will have a chance to sit with her in person before I go into retreat.*

Altar of Longing

Shortly after arriving on the island and before checking in to the retreat center, I went to hear Gangaji speak. I was moved by her presence. Actually, I was enthralled. However, I'd made a determined commitment to the Tibetan Buddhist tradition. Gangaji was basically saying that it was possible to wake up right now in this very moment, that in fact I already was awake; I was just missing the obvious. The Buddhist teachings of the time, however, still advocated a minimum 30 years of devout spiritual practice, and if I worked super hard and was really lucky, then *maybe* I could wake up in this lifetime.

I wrestled with these seemingly conflicting viewpoints because I wanted my best chance at enlightenment, no matter how long it took. I made a "final" decision to check in to the Buddhist center, settled into my little cottage on the cliffs over a wild Hawaiian ocean, and began my spiritual practices. I had no intention of seeing Gangaji again, yet I'd taken the schedule with me of her upcoming *satsangs*. (Loosely translated from the Sanskrit, *satsang* means "association with truth.")

A couple of weeks into the retreat, it was time for Gangaji's next satsang meeting. Would I attend? Those first two weeks at the retreat center had been some of the most precious days of my life. What a relief to finally stop all attempts to find fulfillment in the outside world and devote my attention completely to self-realization.

Chapter 4

Leaving the center to sit with Gangaji felt like being unfaithful to my practices. Again, I was torn. But I had never been very good at denying the force of my desires (obviously), and ultimately I had always trusted my instincts. So I found myself driving halfway across the island to Gangaji's satsang.

Two weeks later, the scenario repeated itself. The same wrestling back and forth in my mind, the same ultimate decision to trust myself. This time, however, I sat on the floor right in front of her and raised my hand to speak.

"Gangaji," I ventured timidly, "when I turn my attention toward discovering the truth of who I am, I touch upon something so bright and so beautiful, I feel like I can't contain it."

Looking directly into my eyes, she said, simply, "You can't contain it—it contains you."

Seven simple words that turned the world on end!

In those few moments of looking into her eyes, I experienced what I can only call "eternity," and I knew it to be myself. Reality had suddenly flipped inside out. It was as though the body/mind/personality I had always believed myself to be took a back seat to the vast infinite awareness that was opening up inside me faster than my mind could track. In fact my mind had stopped completely. I saw with absolute clarity that this ground of being that was revealing itself to itself inside me was actually who and what I am, what sustains this existence yet remains completely independent of it, incorruptible, eternal, and free. I understood all of this in a split second without understanding a thing.

My body trembled and shook as my nervous system grappled in vain for some kind of solid ground. It was as though an internal tsunami were blowing every tidy shoreline of my mind to bits. I did indeed feel stripped naked to the core and completely out of control, including the power to think a single thought.

She gazed at me for some time, taking me in, her eyes an open invitation to drown in an ocean of empty, intelligent love. Finally, she remarked, "My teacher, Papaji, used to share this saying from his teacher, Ramana Maharshi: 'Once an elephant walks through a small tent, that tent is never the same.'" Everyone laughed and Gangaji's attention moved on to the next person.

Twenty years later, I can honestly say that this "tent" has never been the same. The deepening of what was realized in that instant out of time has never really stopped. I knew without a doubt that I'd finally found what I'd hungered for all my life, and so the challenge then became how to stay true to that. The old reality, the conditioned belief in a separate individual who was lost and must find her way home, continued to come and go, yet inevitably it loosened its hold over the years that followed and the unraveling

Chapter 4

continues to this day. As far as I can see, it's a lifetime opening that has no end, requiring honest curiosity, devotion, resolve, truth telling, and the willingness for true inquiry in every moment.

Not everyone needs a teacher to awaken. Yet somehow, I clearly did. I know that I needed this because it's what I got. I'd put out a *very* powerful prayer at the age of sixteen that when the time was exactly ripe, I would meet my teacher. I needed someone from the apparent outside to appear and be the mirror through which I could see myself clearly. And luckily, being the true teacher that she is, she reminded me again and again lest I get caught in projection, "I am your own self." The fact that I was blessed to recognize what was and is being reflected in that mirror is a miracle of grace that flattens me in gratitude to this day.

Back at the retreat center, I returned to my Tibetan practices. However, in the days that followed, those practices began to organically morph into something new. I suddenly realized that chanting words in Tibetan that I didn't even know how to translate made no sense to me whatsoever. The full prostrations that I had been repeating hundreds of times throughout the day, accompanied by Tibetan mantra, now became full bodied, fervent prayers from the depths of my heart—in English. Over and over, as I opened my body in full prostration, I prayed: "Show me the deepest truth. Show me the source of my mind. Deliver me from illusion. Reveal my true nature," and endless supplications along these lines. And the inner revelations just kept coming, the truth kept unfolding; the prayers kept being answered.

For weeks I hiked along the cliffs of East Maui noticing how I was "seeing" everything differently. Oh my God, what beauty! It was as though the force looking out through my eyes was no longer my own ego-centered awareness but God's awareness, eternal and unbound. This new way of seeing was strikingly different at first, like a kind of altered state. Yet the experience eventually normalized, and this sense of "awareness aware of its own infinite vastness" eventually became the new everyday consciousness.

After six of the most precious weeks of this lifetime, I left the retreat center for the final time to join Gangaji on a three-month journey of satsang throughout northern India, Nepal, and Bali. My connection to her and the depth of love and gratitude I feel for her presence in my life are still very much alive in my heart today.

What was once an altar of longing that continually needed tending now needs nothing other than itself. Whenever I find that old familiar yearning rise up and attempt to attach itself to some worldly projection, I know to turn directly into the longing itself and simply surrender to its presence in my heart. I know that it's calling me Home.

Chapter 4

This *something* of huge significance that I had always hungered for is finally revealed to be nothing other than love itself, eternally alive and present and overflowing as the very fabric of existence. In the core of the longing is the ecstasy of love loving its own eternal nature, right here, right now, in my own heart. So simple, so ordinary, so freely available, this unbelievably benevolent causeless love is forever offering itself to us. Whenever my heart starts to burn, whether it be from longing or sadness, fear or grief, it's simply a call to surrender to love, to free-fall, to let myself be consumed by love itself until there is nothing left of *me,* only love. This heart that aches for itself is what makes me human. I bow to it now. A small price to pay, wouldn't you say, for all this magnificence?

If I were to long for anything in this moment it would be for the ability to accurately express what was recognized in that split second of looking into my teacher's eyes, and consequently in the great good fortune of meeting her teacher, Sri H.W.L. Poonja (Papaji), while he was still in the body. But the truth is, all these years later, I still have no satisfactory words for it.

How can one speak of this that is vast beyond belief and present everywhere, in everything, in every moment? How can words convey what is here before any movement in the mind, unborn and yet eternally present? How can one express this thing that's not a *thing,* not an object to be seen in consciousness, nor the subject doing the seeing, but the seeing itself? This language is not a language of the mind; it's a language of the heart. And I can only pray that somehow it might get transmitted through and underneath these words. That somehow through this particular story, this particular flavor of consciousness, you might recognize yourself, and we can meet here forever in the ecstasy of undifferentiated being and revel in our oneness.

© 2013 Shanti Einolander

Shanti is a freelance writer and book editor residing in Ashland, Oregon, and the owner of Clear Light Editorial Services: www.clearlight-edit.com. She is additionally the founder and editor of OneTheMagazine, an online journal bringing the good news of awakening from around the world: www.onethemagazine.com

chapter 5

Answer to a Prayer

Gangaji

One of the most important discoveries of my life was primarily negative, and yet because of it I was brought to what would be revealed as the absolutely essential discovery of my life story.

By the late 1980s I was living a very good life with my husband, Eli. We had moved from Bolinas, CA, over the hill to Mill Valley. We were living in a wonderful little house with a manageable mortgage. We both had fulfilling work, I as an acupuncturist and Eli as a workshop leader and teacher of the Enneagram. And although our relationship still had its trials, we

Chapter 5

recognized each other as life partners. We loved the community we were living in, and we loved each other. And yet...

There was a longing that continued to return. It let me know that however my life looked and felt, however far I had come from my earlier discontent, something deep inside remained unfinished. I couldn't have articulated what was unfinished, since nothing in particular was wrong. Often I would ignore the longing, or categorize it as part of my basic neurotic mental/emotional fixation.

At that time in my life, I was certain that I had discovered all that I needed to know to live a happy, useful life. I had explored many different spiritual and secular paths, and I had discovered many useful tools to appease the yearning in my heart. I knew to meditate to calm my overactive mind. I knew to leave "my" life at the door when helping those who were troubled in some way. I knew that direct and honest communication with my partner was required for a mature relationship. I knew to vote with my conscience and heart at both elections and shops. I knew a lot, but I didn't know what the longing wanted.

Finally I was willing to know that I didn't know. Initially this evoked negative feelings. I thought I should know. I wanted to know. I wanted the uncomfortable feeling in my chest to be cured by all that I knew and practiced. After a brief and miserable period of resisting the truth, I opened my mind to the fact that once again—

Answer to a Prayer

when I told the most naked truth—I was aware of a longing for what I could not even name. I surrendered all pride of accomplishment to the truth that at a fundamental level I remained unfulfilled.

As I had prayed for rescue forty-odd years before, I now prayed to know the truth. Was the truth the glimpses I had had of perfection and beauty, or was the truth the drudgery of life, with glimpses of unbounded love simply a mechanism of brain chemistry to assist this body in getting through life? I didn't know the answer, but I prayed that if there was someone who did know the truth, I might meet and learn from that someone.

It was a different order of prayer than the childish plea I had offered up to Jesus in my younger years. If the truth was that we are doomed creatures of birth-procreation-death, designed only to continue the species in a mechanical universe, I was ready to face that reality. If the truth was something more, I wanted to know that. I wasn't looking for a guru or a savior; I was looking for the true teacher.

Within a year of recognizing that I was ready to face the truth and that I needed help in knowing where and how to look, I met my teacher. Surprising to me, he was a guru, and even more surprising, I had to travel to India to meet him. I had always scoffed at the sentimental, incense-laden devotee relationship to the "guru." I was certain that my Western sophistication put me way beyond what a guru could show me. I wasn't seeking escape in mindless devotion, and I had no patience with name changing and affecting Eastern traditions as a lifestyle. I was wrong. My so-called sophistication and certainty became insignificant with the appearance of my teacher.

Eli had met Papaji first. The letters he wrote to me while visiting this remarkable man were vibrating with love and insight. He wrote me that this man, H.W.L. Poonja, was the real thing. He wrote that he was coming back to get me so that I could meet what we had been searching for our entire lives.

Soon I found myself in India at the bank of the Ganga (Ganges), face-to-face with an enormous force of presence and energy. In the first instant of meeting him, I knew he was the answer to my prayer. He met us at the door of the small house he had rented in Haridwar. As the door opened, I was greeted with an authentic and robust "Welcome, come in!" His deep eyes were flashing with intelligence and joy. I fell in love.

I had no idea what was to follow, but I knew to pay close attention. What was to follow was the discovery of my lifetime. Unknowable to me at the time, the discovery I experienced in his presence, through his grace and guidance, was the opening that naturally led to the profound, truly indescribable shift that finally put me right side up in my life. Meeting him, listening to him, and being with him precipitated a discovery that appeared as a thunderclap in my mind and that is still, quietly now, exploding within me twenty years later.

When I asked my teacher how I could discover the truth—at the time I phrased it as how I could discover freedom—he told me to discover who I am. When I asked him, "How?" he told me to stop everything. He told me to keep still.

Without really understanding how keeping still could answer my questions, I followed his suggestions. As I took his instruction deeper into my consciousness, I recognized how "stop" was a very threatening word to me. I imagined that if I kept still and stopped everything, I would certainly regress and lose all my spiritual accomplishments. I did not want to end up being the person I was back in Clarksdale, Mississippi. I was afraid that if I really stopped, I might have no desire to take care of myself or others. Finally I recognized that in my understanding, to stop meant to die. I was afraid to die. After some useless internal discussions, I did realize that while I might die here in this place, it wasn't likely. I recognized that the fear of death kept me from examining what was here if I truly did keep still. If I stopped searching for anything or hiding from anything, what would I discover?

He told me that what I was looking for was closer than my breath or heartbeat and that it was always here. He said that only

Chapter 5

what is continuously here could truly be called real. He told me to discover what was real. I listened to him and stopped following the thoughts that arose about my future. I stopped thinking about who I was and what I needed. I was still. Astoundingly, I discovered that the seemingly continuous narrative of my thoughts was not continuous after all. I saw clearly that whomever or whatever I thought myself to be changed with passing thoughts and definitions. My definitions of myself were not continuous and therefore not real.

When I withdrew my attention deeper and closer than any thought of myself, or my world, or my accomplishments, or my needs, I discovered conscious space. Space that was conscious! Conscious space that in truth had always been the background of all my different thoughts. Was it continuous? He advised me to find out for myself. I began my investigation by keeping my attention on where thoughts arose from rather than following them out into thought streams.

Thoughts appeared and disappeared and conscious space remained, regardless of the appearance or disappearance of those thoughts. Definitions and descriptions and stories of dazzling variations all had beginnings and endings. I realized that conscious space was the generator and the receiver of all. I discovered that conscious space was both silent and aware. I was conscious of myself as this silent, aware space.

Answer to a Prayer

I discovered myself to be inseparable from whatever appeared in consciousness (body, thoughts, emotions, states of being) and at the same time independent of all forms. I discovered that the duality of our everyday perceptions was enclosed in and penetrated by the unity of conscious space.

Silent, empty, and full too, I found myself to be continuous awareness paradoxically both finding myself and recognizing I had always known myself. This startling—and yet obvious!—discovery was infused with the purest love I had ever experienced. I had loved people and places and objects of beauty, but this love loved with no constraints or needs. I found myself as love in both subject and object.

In the first days and weeks of this astounding discovery, my attention would vacillate between sublime rest in its home and agitated attempts to define or control what was being revealed. It is one of the aims of the human brain, after all, to make sense of our world. When I followed my habit of trying to think what was happening, I found only confusion and denial. When my thoughts took precedence, I would feel a mild panic at losing what a moment before had seemed impossible to lose. I would think "Where is it now? How have I lost it?" And then I would remember Papaji's voice: "Stop. Be still. Recognize who you are." With this encouragement I could stop my habit of searching. Released from seeking to find anything, I found only spacious love.

Finally I became aware of a distinct moment of choice: I could follow thoughts or I could be still. I could identify with reality as generated by the thought process, or I could identify with open, spacious awareness. It was a moment of fear as well as choice. It was a choice between the apparent security of knowing through my evaluations of reality and discovering through opening to reality. Knowing through thinking generated an illusion of safety, but at this point that pseudo-security felt deadening and unsatisfying. Discovering was my choice. Is my choice.

I was familiar with the horror of brainwashing. As a child I had been brainwashed to see people with dark skin as inferior. I had been brainwashed to believe that eternal happiness could be found in finding the right man. I had been brainwashed to think I could achieve everlasting fulfillment by doing some magical "right" thing. Brainwashing is exclusion and requires keeping contradictory information out of consideration. The choice I was making was to open my mind to all.

It didn't seem possible when I thought about it. In fact it wasn't possible when I thought about it. Thoughts demand closing attention to one thing in favor of another. Normally when we are unable to choose which thought to favor we become confused or "cognitively dissonant." We then usually desperately seek a thought that will deliver congruence with our learned view of reality.

I could not find a thought that would support fully opening my mind to all. I could not find a thought that condoned stopping thoughts. Opening was only possible in suspending reliance on any thought as accurate. I was willing. At the same time, I also felt great fear of the possible consequences. I discovered that the willingness to open to what is unknown—and even beyond knowing—is a choice even in the midst of great fear.

What I discovered was not static or dry in any way. How to explain a silence that encloses and saturates the universe? I had read books and accounts about great beings' enlightenment, and I had imagined what that enlightenment must be. In an instant this discovery erased all comparisons of states and degrees of selfhood. I found silent awareness in this form called "me" and also recognized that when this form is long gone, silence, the conscious substance of life—undiminished by any loss—remains. Without the penetrations of life animation, there is no form; yet when the form is finished (or when life animation is finished with the form), life still is.

Realizing and experiencing silent awareness as my own self released a flood of life affirmation. There was a retreat of the fear of death, since life remains after "I" die, and above all I am life. There was laughter that rolled on and on, with tears of bliss and wonder. All questions and all answers were swallowed whole in the direct experience of being conscious of myself as consciousness itself.

And I wasn't brain-dead, or insensate, as I had feared I might be in the moment before surrender. There was a geyser of personal and global insights as my prior knowledge of life was silenced. There was the lucidity of pure sensual experience that found fulfillment in whatever the senses perceived. The exalted blissful state of self-recognition lasted some time, and when the state of bliss passed, there was no longing or regret or sense of losing anything at all. I am was revealed to precede all states, to penetrate all states, and to remain when all states pass away.

In this discovery, there was no question of maintaining anything or keeping anything. Simply being, and being conscious that being is conscious, was the fulfillment. The natural surrender of my seeking mind opened windows of insight daily and even hourly.

One of the most important moments in my time with Papaji was a day when he took us to the market in Haridwar. Indian markets, similar to markets everywhere, are noisy places. They are centers of activity with all types of people shouting and singing or begging people to buy their goods. Added to the noise and the smells was the enervating heat of midday. Earlier that morning we had been sitting peacefully in his small rooms by the river. While at the hot market I had thoughts of wanting to be back in the peace of his rooms with the cooling breeze of the river and the only sound being the whap, whap of the ceiling fan. After internally complaining for a moment or two, I looked up and happened to catch his eye. With startling clarity I seemed to hear him say, "here too." In wonder and bliss, the silence underneath the noise was suddenly obvious. "Underneath the noise" is not precisely correct, but at the time it appeared that way. Later I realize that whatever the noise level, I am here also, and I am silence itself.

Whether listening to Papaji deliver a dharma discourse, hearing him tell a teaching story or some story from his earlier life, going shopping with him for vegetables for the evening meal, or sitting simply in his rooms, each moment was an invitation to silence. Each word was pointing back to and bringing the news of its silent origin.

After leaving Haridwar, I wrote Papaji at least every day, and he answered with beautiful letters of encouragement and confirmation. I was deeply happy and didn't need anything more. Not needing anything more prepared the field of my mind for the lightning bolt that appeared out of the blue one night as Eli and I sat together, reveling in our good luck.

It was some weeks after my visit to Papaji had ended and we were in California, where Eli was leading a group at Esalen. In a

Chapter 5

moment of love and joy with each other, and together appreciating the astounding grace of having met our true teacher, the world as I had known it stopped. When it started again (there was no time involved), I was free. Free of myself as form and free of myself as anything separate from any form. Free of myself as either form or formless. Free of ego and free of egolessness. Free of unenlightenment and free of enlightenment. Fulfillment was here with no search or searcher needed. The story of past suffering had no meaning or power in this instant. All of the scaffolding, all of the support for myself as separate from the bliss of being, fell away in that instant. Peace and love. From that moment, I can say that my life has never been the same. Blessed moment, blessed life, all was truly well.

I looked at Eli and saw we were the same self even in all our differences. Differences and sameness were parts of the wholeness of self. The war between different and same came to an end. The laughter that poured out was the only description I could make.

At a certain point, a couple of years after that, I was aware of a sense of myself as a person starting to slowly return. And I thought, "Oh, no, what does this mean?" because at that point I had been counseling people not to reconstruct themselves after this kind of experience. There was a moment of wondering if this sense of myself meant I had lost anything, but by then I knew enough to check and see. When I did, I saw clearly that the truth that needs no scaffolding was not bothered by any sense or perception of myself as being this human animal, this body-mind configuration. Silent conscious awareness was not bothered by any disappearance of the sense of this form and not bothered by its reappearance.

The fact that the sense of me as form reappeared was actually a teaching for me because it threw me into profound inquiry. And in that inquiry I saw that this sense of being a separate entity appears and disappears all the time, even in a day—for everyone. It's just that until we have an experience of it disappearing, and then discovering the true "I" to still be present, only then do we have the possibility of recognizing that the disappearance or the reappearance doesn't really touch the unmoving truth.

It was at this point I felt myself reincarnating as an ordinary human being. I didn't fight the ordinariness coming back, because I was always aware that whatever came back—an emotion, a sense of me, a negative thought, etc.—it didn't touch what had been revealed in that instant an Esalen.

To this day, I can say that from that moment there has been no lack of resolution and fulfillment. There have been negative states as well as positive. There has been grief as well as joy. There have been trials and there have been defeats, but nothing has dislodged the certainty that who I am includes all.

Chapter 5

And it had always been here. I could look through my life and re-create my personal story, and from the perspective of consciousness recognize myself as pure silent awareness always having been here. The only difference was that now I included myself as awareness along with the objects (I, you, events, emotions, etc.) in awareness.

I could think without being tyrannized by thoughts. I could tell my story without needing it to be anything other than another display of life in form. I recognized that same display of life in all forms, both beautiful and horrid. I recognized that same display in all emotions, in all recoiling and all embracing. I recognized the uncontrollability as well as the undeniability of life awake to itself, and I fell on my knees in gratitude and wonder.

This discovery did not go unnoticed by my teacher—my guru. He was very happy. He supported and confirmed my discovery and always challenged me to more fully, more deeply, more completely discover more. He would say, "See if you can find an end." He also told me that this discovery was so precious that the mind would try to steal it, and as a good thief it would use all its skills and powers to own this precious treasure. He said the mind would be as a wolf in sheep's clothing and that constant vigilance was required.

There were many more discoveries awaiting me as I began to recognize the mandate and force of my thinking mind. There were great challenges waiting and great humbling as I discovered the truth of my guru's warnings. My states ranged from high to low and my ideas about myself paraded in flat deflation and absurd inflation. Yet in both the worst and the best of times, silent awareness, aware of itself, remained the ground of being. Present in all, unmoving and radiant.

I have always failed to accurately describe my self-discovery, although this failure is inseparable from the beauty and the profundity of the discovery. It will not be caught and held by words. It has remained free and alive and undeniable, while I have blissfully attempted to define or describe it.

People have asked me over the years if I am enlightened. Do I see myself as enlightened? I would never deny my ongoing experience of non-duality and fulfillment, which has never left me since that huge and precious moment when all subflooring of doubt was removed. It simply doesn't make sense to define my experience as anything separate from anyone else's. I don't exclude myself from any other. How could I?

So, no, I don't see myself or think of myself in terms of "enlightened being" or "master." Sometimes people give me special titles, but usually those definitions (limitations!) just unravel. When I fell in love with Papaji, I projected all manner of super human characteristics onto him. I think that's the normal course when we fall in love. Then I actually had the opportunity of seeing him in ordinary situations—irritated with somebody for not answering a question correctly, or misunderstanding somebody, not hearing them exactly. By the time I met Papaji, he was in eighties and was having some pain in his body, and pain often gives rise to crankiness. Later I read about Ramana, the great Indian sage and Papaji's guru, who was cranky, too, toward the end, when his body was suffering from cancer. It allowed me to open my mind to see that there's room for these moods or states of mind that we have determined keep us unenlightened; and that all states are finally superficial, simply functions of body and emotions.

There is peace and bliss, but what is more essential about this discovery is its pure aliveness. In a completely real sense, it is not something that happened to me; it is the discovery of who I am. It is simultaneously the background, foreground, and middle ground. It is pure life that is constant, regardless of what is born or what dies. More importantly, for our meeting through these words, it is the life that exists in each of us. It will leave our particular forms someday, but in this instant we can recognize that life is the constant. Forms of all kind come and go. People, thoughts, emotions, sensations, states, internal and external events of every kind come and go. Life remains. We can each, and all, recognize ourselves as life, conscious of itself.

Answer to a Prayer

© 2011 Gangaji

Above article was extracted from Gangaji's award-winning book, *Hidden Treasure: Uncovering the Truth in Your Life Story*, published by Jeremy P. Tharcher/Penguin of The Penguin Group: New York, 2011.

Other books include *The Diamond in Your Pocket: Discovering Your True Radiance; Your Are THAT!* and *Freedom and Resolve: The Living Edge of Surrender*

Gangaji is dedicated to the recognition of peace and freedom inherent in the core of all being. She is supported by her Foundation's global network of volunteers. Gangaji has met with hundreds of thousands of people from all walks of life in open meetings and retreats for the past twenty years. Visit her website: www.gangaji.org

chapter 6

When It's Personal

Christine Horner

Author Christine Horner shares the life circumstances that led to what she calls "a crucifixion of the ego." As she writes, "Though life is holistically impersonal, as part of the Divine Paradox there is also a personal aspect to life. My ability to transcend the personal came through personal experience; therefore, much of what I write here comes from direct perception rather than conventional proof."

After a lifetime of an on and off again love affair with God, bouncing through various religions, in 2006 I turned my life

Chapter 6

over to God. Literally, I gave my bodily existence over to God to know Truth, accepting that it could even mean my physical death. The human constructs of what God was according to my own personal culture and conditioning had become so unsatisfactory and ridiculous in my mind, after spending much time in Nature and in contemplation, I could no longer accept those constructs. Nothing less than the Truth was acceptable to me beyond this point. With Buddha and Jesus as my inspiration, I told God to "put me on the fast track."

It was shortly after that I wrote a poem called, *The Gift,* not fully comprehending the magnitude of those words and where they would lead me. On top of the world and ready for anything, my cup overflowing with positive energy and affirmations, my life utterly and devastatingly...fell apart. Broke with $20 left in my pocket and groceries in the refrigerator from my ex so I could feed the kids, I was forced to make the decision to call my family across the country to send money so I could pack the car to travel back to the Midwest—the last place I wanted to go back to—as it meant I would once again be separated from my son.

A month later my grandma, who had been a rock in my life, passed away. A family disagreement led to my estrangement from my entire family during that same time, and then finally, weeks before Christmas the same year, my 11-year-old daughter was diagnosed with cancer—a brain tumor.

Her father and my son, living across the country, rushed to be with her for brain surgery. Unable to afford to commute across the country regularly, my daughter and I braved the chemo/radiation and many weeks in the hospital, for the most part, alone. It was when I was up all night with a child vomiting into a bucket that the channels of clarity began to open wide for me. I spent much time writing and working from my laptop plugged into a hospital Ethernet cable as my daughter slept in her hospital bed or rested at home.

I felt such purpose with this greater clarity. I desired to save the world and even formed a non-profit foundation with the last vestiges of the inheritance I received from beloved Grandma.

As my inspiration felt divine, my hard work was sure to be rewarded; supporting not only my daughter and me, but allowing me to share with those that I loved and had supported me in the past.

It wasn't to be so.

The sustenance and partnerships I had hoped to bring to fruition toward alleviating the world of its self-created suffering never materialized. Despite "doing" all that I could to keep

Chapter 6

"negative thinking" at bay and the positive affirmations of myself as part of the Infinite flowing, I began the final death spiral into the abyss of total darkness through an extended Dark Night of the Soul.

My small business consulting clients had long since dried up. As my daughter needed continual medical care for a persistent hormone elevation that rendered her medical team unable to declare her in remission, finding regular employment was nearly out of the question; unless I lied my way through the interview process which I finally succumbed to doing.

No matter what I did, the results were always the same—no channel opened up to end the hell I was going through, though a friend did take us in for a while and another friend lent me some money, which in the end only delayed the inevitable.

I sold everything I owned piece-by-piece. I meditated, I prayed, I read everything I could get my hands on, I tried to BE—and I waited. I waited some more for that miracle that never came. The Universe had always generously supported me in the past; why was every stream now dry and barren?

I lost my apartment and my daughter was separated from me, moving in with her best friend's family and I was unable to hug my teenage son who lived across the country, for two years. Thank goodness for Internet video chat.

It was this time that I was left hanging on my own personal cross, crying out, "Why have you forsaken me?"

I had had faith. I had believed. I'd done the work *and* I'd dedicated my life to God and serving humanity. How could this be happening to me?

I couldn't find God anywhere that I looked. I felt numb and dead inside. I'd never felt so abandoned. This was my crucifixion of the ego. In that some people have a health-related physical near-death experience, this was as near death as I was to get as I contemplated how I could gracefully bow out of the lives of my children without causing them irreparable damage and end the depths of my despair. The crazy thing was I couldn't even shed any tears over the situation. There was literally nothing left inside, except, finally...total surrender of everything I thought I had ever understood about life.

I wore a brave face and kept my affairs as private as I possibly could, until one day I told God that I was done with this experience of living in my car. Apparently, Life Itself agreed. Life brought a kind stranger into my life who became the clichéd trickle of light at the end of the tunnel. When this sweet man, who bought my last possession off of Craigslist, finally figured out why I was spending my days at the library, the coffee shop, and the park, he and his wife immediately took

Chapter 6

me into their home. Eventually, my daughter also came to stay while I worked to get back on my feet.

Throughout this period of "wandering the desert" in empty hopelessness, my life as I had known it was deconstructed, including most of what I had previously clung to as precious. I was done with books and teachings. I was even done with Jesus and Buddha, whom I had begged, even screamed at, to show up and tell me what I wasn't getting. *All* of my beliefs were deconstructed, even the new ones I'd replaced the old ones with, including letting go of any egoic idea of saving the world, letting go of any concept that I was special in any way, and, eventually, letting go of any belief in a personal *me*. The depth of this letting go allowed me to see that *I AM Life Itself.*

Surrender must be so deeply experienced that even hope, a concept rooted in an imaginary future and a personal self, must fall away. All teachings and all teachers must fall away. Every concept we are still grasping at for safe harbor must leave until we are utterly naked before God, who is none other than Creation Itself.

Here's the miracle I discovered: True freedom is not about what the egoic, personal self "gets." One cannot carry one single item of baggage through the doorway, not even the personal self. The only way through is emptiness.

When It's Personal

Throughout this period of the emptiness revealing itself, I had many epiphanies. I realized that God/Life had never abandoned me because there was never any outside deity looking down over me in the first place, making judgment calls and therefore decisions on my behalf. Life, by its very nature, supports life, even in this situation when a loving universe didn't look like I thought it should.

I came to understand that on the local level, it appears as if I have free will, but that as part of the tapestry of life, Life is just "Life-ing," and the concept of free will is rooted in a limited point of view. Is a drop of water ever really separate from the ocean? If I have free will, then separation is real.

When the awareness comes to the forefront that a choice is to be made, no matter what fork in the road is taken, it is done by Life Itself.

Ultimately there is no separate "me," as I am the imperishable absolute behind the relative, the BE-ing behind human thought that is timeless and eternal. "I" is the light. As Creation Itself, we are forever whole and the entire relative world is our projection of thought, making us its creator.

Many people confuse this concept with the egoic idea that you can manifest all that you desire by your thoughts alone. Life manifests life. Whether your individuated idea of what life should look like appears in your physical reality depends on whether or not it supports life as a whole.

I share this with you not to draw attention to myself, but rather to first comfort you in that it isn't necessary to go through a near-death-experience or financial devastation to discover who you really are as the Infinite. (Neither does your newfound discovery exempt you from hardship.)

Though many are going through their own personal crucifixions of the ego or dark nights of the soul as a unique expression of the Infinite, how your life appears is one-of-a-kind; no one will have your exact experience.

When you accept and love yourself unconditionally, essentially forgiving yourself—for there is no one *"out there"* to forgive—you see that life conspires to support you. You see that what you do is not as important as the fact that you BE, and that to know what you be, you must inquire within. When connected to your BE-ing, what you do arises as an expression of your BE-ingness as part of the tapestry of Life and is not the goal itself. The ego's need to claim do-ership, ownership, or exclusivity is no longer a part of who you are. The idea of a separate self even begins to fall away, like so much unnecessary debris. Living and breathing from your radiance, you become a light unto the world, and you joyfully offer your magnificence to the world...as a GIFT.

© 2013 Christine Horner

Founder of What Would Love Do Int'l, media arm, In the Garden Publishing and Bodhi UniversiTree, Christine Horner is dedicated to the advancement of human consciousness. Christine is the author of the acclaimed and ground-breaking *What Is God? Rolling Back the Veil*, merging science and spirituality, and *The Gift*. Christine has been featured on The Sheila Show, Science to Sage Radio and in OM Times Magazine online. Visit Christine at: www.ChristineHorner.com, www.Facebook.com/hornerchristine, www.Twitter.com/itgpublishing

chapter 7

Bushwhacked by Grace

Sahaja Jaeger

There are times in life when we ask questions without any real comprehension of what we are asking for. We can ask a simple question and we don't realise the potential enormity in the answer. The question of "who am I?" is one of those questions.

I was inspired to write my story for people whose experiences of Grace may have come with unexpected and incapacitating consequences to the form. Through telling this story perhaps I can offer support and encouragement for embracing the unknown, for finding greater peace by staying true to what was revealed, and in a very human sense, for knowing that you are not alone. Finally, is the

Chapter 7

possibility and invitation to discover that whatever is happening is just right for you.

Back in 2000, I had a successful career in terms of how our society views it. I was a very dynamic, active person, respected by management and customers, in a senior management position of a large science and technology organisation. My marriage, however, had come to a liberating end, and in recognising behaviours that were not serving me or the people I loved in my life, I wanted to change. I wanted to know who I really was. I was an intellectual person, and for the first time in my life, I asked for counselling help, which opened the door to an adventure of spiritual discovery. I was also directed towards vipassana meditation and shamanism. In another three years I was really happy in a new relationship and the direction of my working life felt as if I was right on track. My own internal investigations and growth were being reflected in what I was able to contribute back to the workplace and it felt really positive.

In 2003, all of that dramatically changed. At the conclusion of a shamanic retreat, whilst sitting with friends over a relaxed dinner and a glass of wine, I opened into a spontaneous altered-state experience. The best way I could describe it was the sense that I was leaving my body. I was resisting and holding onto my friends in terror of the potential of not returning to this body. Within a few minutes I could see that this was futile, I could not stop this. So, with resolve I told myself, "Well, I wanted to know who I really am, if I'm committed to that, then this is it," and I surrendered the fear of death. Without that resistance, almost instantaneously, mind and body, time and space, no longer existed. Given the limitation of words and the impossibility of the mind's capacity to describe what was discovered, the best way I can convey what was revealed is that of alive, boundary-less, blackness. Without mind and body there were no sensations or emotions to describe the ground of being from which all of this known 'trance' of life on earth and the universe arises. My true nature had been revealed.

When 'my' mind and sense of a separate self arose again, and I found myself back in the body, I recognised that life was not as I had known it before. I had to learn how to use my body again and my whole perception of reality was not as it had been. I could not speak properly, I needed assistance to move, I was hypersensitive to my environment and there was no defence from its onslaught. Light, sound, the emotions of those around me, and the electromagnetic emissions that we take for granted around the household, all bombarded my system, creating not only optical and migrainal pain, and what I affectionately later called energetic 'spac attacks' (fits of shaking), but also what I came to know as energetic heart pain. Even when I looked around me, it was as if I was looking at a surreal scene. It took seven days before I had enough control of my body

Chapter 7

that I was provided assistance in returning to my home, thus beginning the most challenging few years of my life. For all that you will read below, I have no regrets, and immense gratitude for what was revealed.

Initially I had no way of retaining my own energy or keeping harmful energies out. Without assistance, I could not look after myself. I discovered how much energy it takes to think, to read, to defend against the unseen radiation from telephones, computers, appliances, televisions, and city living in general—all too much for this system to bear, so exhausting and the exposure so painful.

For many months, most of my day was spent meditating on the couch. That was all the energy I had, enough for some basic functions. My only moments of nourishing salvation, and a rest from defending against external aggravators, were excursions into nature well away from the city, where I could at least experience a semblance of former physical capacity, and I was able to go for a walk. On being brought back into the city, I'd be a shaking mess til the body once again adjusted to the relative protection of the house and the city energy.

During this time there was a relentless arising of everything I had formally 'swept under the carpet' and not met. Unfelt emotions, unresolved demons of belief, concepts, and story, all came calling along with further beautiful glimpses of grace. This time, however, the glimpses of grace occurred with the 'trance' of what we call reality still playing like a hologram before my eyes. Twelve months further down the track, there was a second even more incapacitating spontaneous experience.

In all, 20 months went by before I finally found a metaphysical practitioner who was able to assist me, through the use of trance, to begin the long journey of my body's recovery. His description of my circumstances was to use a metaphor of a human being as an egg: I was wearing the yolk on the outside of my shell, with no protection from outside energy and no way to hold my own in.

During this time there were great challenges for me and for those trying to support me. For the medical profession and workplace, this fell well outside common experience, conventional thinking, and knowledge. There was beautiful support for which I am deeply grateful to the many people who helped me to survive and to be supported where I could not manage for myself in this society. I had no one in my life who could really validate what had happened or knew how to help me beyond encouraging me to meet what arose. I was still spiritually immature when this began and in need of looking to the outside for confirmation and answers. I was faced with professional people labelling me in ways that I could only let go of or risk sinking into severe depression. I had to let go of what all the people who knew me thought of me or believed about

Chapter 7

my circumstances. One of the hardest things to let go of was my own search for validation and understanding.

Something like four years down the track, I knew beyond doubt that life was my teacher, but I felt stuck and saw that I needed to let go of this stance and be willing to find a teacher. It was then that I pulled a book off the shelf that had been sitting there unread for five years. It was here I found Gangaji in the book by Amber Terrell, *Surprised by Grace.* My experience of life matched what Gangaji spoke of and I felt great resonance with her. Within a few months Gangaji was scheduled to be in Australia and so I booked straight away, and with her came her husband, Eli Jaxon-Bear. During this first meeting she pointed me to a book called *A Stroke of Insight* by Jill Bolte Taylor. It was here that I finally discovered that people can have experiences that result with the symptoms of a stroke without having had the stroke. I recognised in Jill's own account what I had been through, without anyone in the medical profession even considering this possibility. Like her experience of the physical stroke, it took me 7-8 years to blessedly recover to the quality of life I now enjoy, with some functionality still not as it was before, but manageable.

It became very clear to me that for each and every one of us, our experiences of Grace are not to be compared to those of others. It is a mystery how, when, and where it happens and how it is experienced. There is no prerequisite to be doing anything in particular or sitting in a sacred place. For me, both major events occurred in very ordinary circumstances in rural Australia, the second beginning simply as I was walking across my yard to pack the car. Another occurred simply as I was sitting at home. That being said, there were also other experiences initiated through direct experience of being supported in satsang with teachers. Being understood by others, as well as my own validation, aren't needed by who I truly am, only by the one who thinks it is in control, and tries to find some way to understand and to know, so as to feed that illusion of being in control, to have the safety of the known, and to maintain connection with perceived 'others.' Grace reveals itself in many varied ways, and it introduces a further veiling layer of misconception and potential suffering to believe or expect that it will happen for us the way it does for others, or by doing something in particular, or by practising what others have done, or by projecting that 'way' onto others. Who you are is already actually here, looking exactly as it is, both within and as the body you are perceiving the world through, just as you are, right in this moment. It is also in empty space and every thing you perceive to be 'outside' your form.

I have come to know that the life that is living these forms brings all that is supportive to help us discover or more fully recognise who we truly are. You can trust that if practices will benefit or serve, then life will introduce them in some way. If there is an appropriate teacher or pointer to guide you, they will be revealed, and by teacher I mean everyday ordinary folk as well as those public figures past and present assisting people in their spiritual discoveries. Life is satsang and satsang is life, 24 hours a day and seven days a week. As I have heard Eli say, "Everything is used." In my own life I have discovered that even to trust makes little sense anymore, and is not required or needed. There simply just is what is unfolding. Life/love is as it is, a formless continuum that remains free of any human experiences, and yet human experience is included. Who is it that needs to trust? For me the one who experiences or feels the need to trust is the one who is surrendered. Over time I learned that the mind has no trustworthy or true idea of what is needed, so the simplest is to surrender to whatever presents itself to be fully met and experienced. It became apparent that anything that came from the minds machinations was not to be believed.

Through both Gangaji and Eli, and with the use of Eli's teachings of *The Enneagram of Liberation* and its associated skilful means, I have come to know my true self more and more fully. This machine of form no longer runs the way it used to, and when it does, it is not taken personally. The planning, scheming, analysing, projecting mind no longer has my full attention. It is with ever-growing loving devotion that my attention is pointed toward the alive presence from which all arises, and from there I await the words to speak and the effortless action to unfold. I love this emptiness that is not empty, this that cannot really be described, and as that love grows there is only more support to knowing it even more fully, veils dissolving, revealing a new perception, never ending, but always the ground unchanging. Life is a spontaneous mystery, and there are no more labels about how the story of this life should look or play out, no defined roles. I am only ever who I am, as I am, with no right or wrong way as to how that will look for this form.

Life has become simpler. Whether it looks like a person cooking in the kitchen, painting for children, or using the skilful means as taught to me by Eli to help point others to who they really are—no difference, really—who I am is always here. Love is living this form and I am deeply grateful for the discovery of my true nature. It has become clear to me that the only way to possibly express my gratitude is to surrender ever more completely, and to continuously recognise what is distracting my attention, and bring it back to my beloved—love's will be done.

If I could offer one piece of wisdom to take away from here, it would be to come to know your true nature through your own self-inquiry, willingness, discovery, and experience. Let go of all expectation, don't believe the words I have written, or any words

Chapter 7

spoken or written by anyone at any time in the earth's history. If you can keep your attention on the source of all experience and to where it all returns, then all is simply as it is…you.

Blessings to all of you in opening to your own inquiry and experiencing ever-growing fulfilment in this heart of life. May all beings know their true nature.

© 2013 Sahaja Jaeger

If you are moved to contact Sahaja, or would like to know more about the Enneagram of Liberation, what it is, what it offers, or the possibility of a 'true friend' session, please use the contact form: http://truenaturewithsahaja.com

chapter 8

Untamable Fire

Amoda Maa Jeevan

For every person that awakens, there's a different picture. We often look at spiritual teachers, enlightened masters, mystics and saints, and try to model our enlightenment on what we see. We say, "Ah, this is what it looks like!" and the ego tries to make sense of it according to its own predispositions. Inevitably, the outer expression of enlightenment is colored by history, geography and biography. The stillness of Ramana Maharshi looks very different to the crazy wisdom of Chogyam Trungpa, and the secular life of one of today's non-duality teachers looks very different from the mystical life of Jesus. And yet we're often fooled into packaging

Chapter 8

what we call "truth," and then believing that this package is something we can claim for ourselves. It's a kind of spiritual reward system that keeps us on the wheel of seeking. But truth—like love—is uncontainable. It is untamable, unconditional, and universal. True awakeness cannot be bought or copied or manufactured; it can only be discovered as that which recognizes itself in everything.

Perhaps because of my life circumstances, my personality, or my karmic predispositions—I cannot possibly know why and it doesn't actually matter why—that which discovered itself through me was revealed in the midst of an extended "dark night of the soul." It was totally unexpected and radically changed the landscape of my inner life. In time, it also altered the landscape of my outer life in ways I could not have imagined. At the core of all of this was a death of "me" as a story-maker.

My story has many twists and turns, as do most stories of redemption. The circumstances surrounding my birth were traumatic and shrouded in secrecy and shame, as were my early years. I never knew my real father and my mother and her family covered up the fact that he left when I was born. The social and cultural disgrace was a heavy burden for my mother, as was her history of abuse and abandonment, and she created a story around it that was far from the truth. When I was born, she was sent to a different country to be married to a man she did not know. I believed he was my father and when, at the age of 13, I found out that he wasn't, my whole world fell apart. Life continued to bring me many unexpected changes that caused me to question who I was and where I came from. Much later, as an adult, this uncertainty about my ancestral roots would form the bedrock of a path of self-inquiry; but as a young child and adolescent, I experienced these unwelcome events as shocks to my delicate nervous system. Some of these shocks were so dramatic they rendered me mute for periods of time and included emotional and physical violence, sexual abuse, abrupt changes in schooling, the sudden onset of war in the Middle East where we lived for a while, a dramatic evacuation by the military, the loss of all possessions, parental divorce, family lies, and probably a few other things! All of these events contributed to a deep sense of shame and confusion but which would eventually become the catalysts for my spiritual search.

Communication was always a problem in my home, as neither of my parents spoke fluent English, nor did they speak each other's language. On the other hand, I could read and write only English and I spoke it perfectly. I suppose I must have been confused, but this strange set-up was my normality. What wasn't so normal was the strictness of my upbringing: I never could work out why the adults in my life were so strict; it just was that way. Playing with other children outside of school hours was forbidden, as was playing

Chapter 8

with dolls and stuffed toys. Birthdays and Christmas' were solemn affairs in which the most exciting gifts, other than pajamas, socks, and school uniforms, were a set of colored pencils and a drawing pad.

The denial of these basic childhood rights cut right to my core, and I came to the conclusion that I was flawed and I deserved to be punished by never getting what I wanted. I felt impure and unworthy, so I prayed to Jesus most nights to cleanse me of my sins, and I prayed to the Holy Mother to take care of me. Unsurprisingly, as an only child with no friends, I became isolated, introverted, and I retreated into a fantasy world that was my only solace. I spent endless hours creating a secret fantasy life in which every detail was mapped out in incredible intricacy, where not only did I have parents who totally adored and understood me, but I also had every single toy and dress I ever wanted, a list of friends who celebrated me, a fascinating life of adventure, and a sense of magic that took me to faraway lands and even into outer space. But this imagined perfect world in which I was perfectly safe, perfectly loved, and perfectly happy was never now, it was always in the future...and the future never came.

Eventually, my escape into utopia became a prison. By the time I was a teenager, I had effectively shut myself off from feeling the full vibrancy of life. In fact, I had shut myself off from feeling, period. When I left home at 17 to go to University, instead of feeling happy and free as I'd expected, I became depressed and felt socially inadequate, and my frequent attempts at suicide led me to believe I'd end up in a mental asylum. I was sent to various psychotherapists and psychiatrists, but none of them could help me. I just sat looking at the floor unable to utter a word. My boyfriend at the time called it "the bell jar," as in the title of Sylvia Plath's famous autobiographical novel of the late 60's. Sylvia Plath committed suicide shortly after its publication. I understood intellectually what "the bell jar" referred to, but I denied that it had anything to do with what was going on for me.

Surprisingly, in spite of this internal landscape of darkness, I threw myself with great vigor into my academic studies. I stopped believing in Jesus or the Holy Mother as my saviors, and I invested my hope of salvation in the achievement of a Doctorate of Psychology. The seeking mechanism that had fueled my earlier fantasy world of perfection was still the driving force of my life, only this time it drove me to work incredibly long hours almost to the exclusion of anything else. I struggled for 12 years against many odds, and then over a period of just a few months, unexpectedly and dramatically—as was the theme of my story—the whole edifice of my life collapsed. At the age of 28, I found myself homeless and penniless. Not only did my academic career come to an abrupt end, but my long-term boyfriend left me, my home was repossessed, I

Chapter 8

became financially bankrupt and without any income, and almost all my material possessions were taken from me. As a result of all these losses in quick succession, I also lost my pride, my confidence, and my dream of a personal utopia. Every single vestige of identity invested in being an academic high-flyer, an urban super-woman, an ideal girlfriend, or any other picture of perfection, came tumbling down. It was both devastating and a great relief. Without the usual attachments of modern-day life, and without the burden of trying to "be somebody," I found myself fully open to living in the present. I also found myself naturally drawn to asking the question that had been sown in my early childhood: "Who am I?"

The next seven years were spent in deep inner exploration. A series of mystical and visionary experiences came without warning and were the catalysts for my subsequent immersion in meditation, primal therapy, rebirthing, metaphysics, psychedelics, and a myriad of psycho-spiritual methods. I was particularly drawn to Buddhist and Zen meditation practices and devoted my attention to these. The sanctuary of inner silence seemed very familiar to me and, unlike my brief encounter with TM during my university days, which had left me horrified at the intensity of voices in my head, I fell into this space effortlessly. I also loved reading, so I devoured as many traditional and contemporary spiritual books as I could, and along the way I visited various spiritual teachers. But I quickly discovered that truth is a fresh discovery not a learnt wisdom, so I didn't stick with anything or anyone for too long. In any case, I wasn't looking for enlightenment; I was looking for happiness.

My search for happiness eventually led me to India and to the ashram of the revolutionary mystic, Osho. Although Osho had left his body just a few years earlier, something deep within me stirred, and I opened to the unconditional love in his invisible presence. I fell in love with his rebellious spirit, absorbed his words, gave my totality to his unorthodox meditative techniques, and bathed in the silence of solitude for several months. I was consumed by an inner fire that blasted my heart wide open, and I willingly surrendered to the tantric mystery of existence. By leaving behind the relative safety of my home and my relationship, I faced my fear of aloneness and discovered that love is at the core of everything. Somehow this realization allowed me to see through the identification with form, and I stopped searching for a teacher or a teaching; instead, life itself became the guru. For the first time in my life, I felt a certain freedom and joy. Perhaps the many hours spent screaming, shouting, and shaking my way through different forms of psychotherapy had helped me let go of some of my emotional baggage. Perhaps I had tasted the truth of emptiness. Whatever the reason, I left India feeling reborn and with a new name, Amoda Maa Jeevan, which means "living a joyous life."

Chapter 8

Back in England, I started teaching transformational workshops and developed my own unique method of "ecstatic meditation," which included breathwork, movement, and music. I was growing beyond my limitations and life was good. I was no longer looking for a spiritual high, but there was a subtle seeking still going on that had to do with relationship. I still held a deep belief that I needed relationship to give me something I hadn't yet found in myself. I needed another to make me feel complete, to confirm my worthiness by giving me love in the form of a perfect relationship. I clung to the idea that a soul mate would fulfill all my inner and outer dreams. Unfortunately, the man I'd decided was my soul mate didn't conform to my ideas of a perfect life, and so we raged, battled, and hurt each other, whilst passionately loving each other, for 10 years. One day, seemingly out of the blue, our relationship exploded and there was no mending it. I harnessed enough courage within myself to walk away. Over a period of three years, I grieved intensely, healed my broken heart with all manner of therapies and bodywork, and eventually learnt to enjoy my own company and the freedom of living alone.

However, in the silent space of solitude, a deeper wound revealed itself: a profound existential fear that I'd been abandoned by God. I felt empty and incredibly alone. As I had done many years before, I began sinking into a black hole, except this time I had enough insight to recognize the call to true freedom. I saw that I wanted to be free of the story of "me" and I was willing to give up my need for love, relationship, happiness, enlightenment—and even the need for any certainty—for this that I could not name. I had no idea how to do this. There was no teacher, no road map, no instruction manual, and no imagination of what I was falling in to. But I trusted the gentle yet insistent impulse to be still and to stop running away, to not follow—as I had done a million times before—the familiar contortions of my mind, and to meet directly in naked awareness the most primal of fears: annihilation. I opened to not-knowingness and allowed myself to die into this. And in this dying, all notions of self dissolved into emptiness. I suppose I expected a kind of cold no-thingness, but instead an incredible joy arose. Without labeling it or packaging it or re-investing any identity in it, the emptiness revealed a luminosity of being. It had always been here, and, contrary to appearances, I had never been separate from this.

From that moment on, I became a lover of what is, unafraid to get right up close and intimate with whatever appears in my experience. My suffering became my doorway to freedom. This freedom now looks nothing like I had imagined it to be. I'm often asked: "How is your life different after awakening?" I can only say that life goes on as it always has. It is utterly unchanged, and yet, in meeting everything as it is, everything has changed.

Chapter 8

Today, 10 years later, the waves of phenomenal existence called "my story" continue. Sometimes the sea is stormy; sometimes it is as calm as a millpond. Sometimes there is pain, hardship, and unpleasant emotions. There is an exquisite sensitivity to every nuance of movement, and yet nothing touches the pristine silence at the core of it all. The radiant jewel that is this silence continues to illuminate those places in my body-mind vehicle that are still holding ancient patterns that do not serve the bigger picture of love. It's an on-going demolition project in which everything that is not true is destroyed. It happens effortlessly and there's nothing I have to do to make it happen. It is ordinary and it is graceful.

I do not know what awakening will look like in you. All I know is that this awakening hinges on your genuine desire for awakening. If it is to flower in you, you must truly want liberation from everything that is false in you, you must want to give yourself totally to the inquiry into what is true beyond all inherited concepts, ideas, and beliefs. When the flame of this desire becomes an untamable fire, it flips a switch inside of you and the direction of your destiny is irrevocably altered. It's like turning on the light only to discover that you are this light. This in itself is extra-ordinary. Even though you may have heard the words a thousand times, nothing can prepare you for the naked reality that is revealed. And yet the living experience of this revelation is very ordinary: you have simply re-discovered the innocent wholeness of your essential nature. It's the you that never was and never will be separate from anything at all. This discovery is the end of suffering and the beginning of freedom.

© 2013 Amoda Maa Jeevan

Amoda Maa Jeevan is a spiritual teacher, author, and the founder of the Foundation for Conscious Change. The above article is an extract from her third book, *Radical Awakening*. To find out more about Amoda, to contact her, or for a schedule of events, visit her website at: www.AmodaMaaJeevan.com

chapter 9

When Love Comes Into Form
Scott Kiloby

I had a profound awakening experience in 2007. The only word that describes that experience, for me, is pure love. It felt like the entire universe was drenched in love. Love was everything, because there was nothing left of separation. I laughed for days, while looking back at how the pettiness of self had reared its head all those years in my 20's and 30's, with my fears, resentments, emotional reactions, and feelings of awkwardness and alienation in relationships.

In that moment, it seemed as if in one fell swoop the entire story had been lifted. There were no separate forms. No Scott, no

Chapter 9

partner, no parents, no friends. Nobody. Pure formlessness. And I thought I was done or there was no one to be done, as they say. If there would have been a certificate for achieving the be-all, end-all realization, I would have taken it and hung in on my wall. Done, finished...it's all over. Enlightenment is here...so I thought....

But that wasn't the end. It was just the beginning. In some way that was not fully conscious, the love felt like "too much." It's as if a part of me began to find little ways to distract myself from it, and to suppress or push down the bliss that wanted to easefully flow throughout my body as the contraction of self released. The distractions were ohhh soooo subtle, not even recognizable. I wasn't consciously distracting myself. The experience of no self was fully here. I saw no self whenever I looked. But the distractions appeared anyway, right out of the conditioning of my body and mind.

It started with really subtle addictions to fairly innocuous things. Not the big stuff like heroin or alcohol. Instead it was coffee, sugar, sex, and for a short period of time, tobacco. Each little addiction would obscure the love in its own little way, making my body feel slightly dull and contracted in certain spots.

And then there were the relationship issues. No big blowouts. No screaming fits of rage, depression, or conflict. Just little eddies of emotional reaction coming from a leftover sense of "I'm unlovable." These weren't big stories that came trumpeting in with lots of pomp and circumstance, but more like a sting in the stomach here or a feeling of fear there, when that very old story of unlovability would be triggered. It was mainly my partner that seemed to be able to trigger these tender spots.

How could this have happened? I thought I realized that life is pure love? How could I still be experiencing these small pockets of separation? These questions popped up.

The answer to all those questions, as I've said, is that the love felt like "too much." At first these addictions and triggers seemed like regression, until I realized instead that these were all opportunities. Life had started anew back in 2007, but the body and mind found ways to hang out in old patterns. I knew then that all I had to do was take a more focused look. No more self-deception. No more stories of someone who is enlightened. Looking needed to happen. This love just needed to find its way into the human form of Scott.

I did that looking with what I call the "living inquiries." Way before I trained facilitators, I was using the inquiries to untie the knots of these addictions and relationship stories. The inquiries were my own little private tool. I was like a child who had discovered a new toy and I was so eager to play. And as each story unraveled, and each pain was felt and each addiction was released,

Chapter 9

the love surfaced again in full force. It started to infuse every form, every manifest thing in my experience. This time it was not pure formlessness. It was coming into every aspect of life, every relationship, every behavior, every reaction, everything. At first, I saw the thought again, "This is too much." But instead of giving it any attention, I relaxed and looked. I looked for the self that was unlovable in every relationship trigger, especially when the quips of my partner would bring a sting. I couldn't find that unlovable "me" anywhere, not even in these really subtle triggers that, perhaps, many people don't even bother looking into even after a big awakening experience.

As the addictions died their sweet little deaths and the unlovable story was all but a distant memory, I remember seeing how innocent it all is. It's so innocent that the body and mind would try to protect itself from a love that big, a love that has no boundaries, a love that infuses every form. Of course the body and mind would do this, if it felt as if the love was "too much." And of course that kind of love is too much for a self. A self can't hold it or do anything with it. The self is the antithesis of this big love. The self is just a series of mechanisms designed to protect itself from feeling such a natural flow of loving energy. As all this unfolded, the story of being enlightened died too. That story too was a form of self-protection. It began to seem like a distant memory, irrelevant completely.

When Love Comes Into Form

Today the love is no longer too much. It's just simple love. Really simple! The love seemed big in that experience in 2007 because it was like a bright light switching on after years of darkness. But once the light is on and it begins to illuminate all the small pockets of darkness, it is no longer big. It only seemed too big when I, the self, was trying to hold it, contain it, or make room for it. When that stopped happening, it turned to a simple love that infuses everything, a love that doesn't announce itself as special or enlightened or even universal. It's too simple for all that mystical wordiness and self-aggrandizing. And it's not just formlessness, as it seemed before. It's not other-worldly. It's form too. It's this world, these relationships, these people, this life. It is right here, everywhere. It's not just realized in an experience. It's lived. It's a love that just says "hi" with a smile to the stranger behind the gas station register. It's a love that finds no trigger when my partner makes a little quip. It's a love that feels warm compassion for someone who is struggling. It's a love that makes room for everything, even pain, fear, and conflict. It's a love that just keeps quiet about itself, except for moments like this when I write about it. It's a love that is not too much at all. And it's as much about being a person, as illusory as that is, as being nobody at all.

© 2013 Scott Kiloby

Chapter 9

Scott Kiloby is an author and international speaker on the subject of awakening and addiction. To learn more about his work with the Living Inquiries, visit his website: www.kiloby.com. His latest books are *Living Realization: Your Present Experience... As It Is*, and *Living Relationship: Finding Harmony with Others*.

chapter 10

The Last Place I Thought to Look

Hillary Larson

*There is a mysterious occurrence
in certain people's lives,
whereby in a moment of grace,
the possibility of a truer life is revealed.
— Gangaji*

I was first asked to write an article about my recovery from drugs and alcohol, which began as a result of an intervention that was done on me back in 1986. To be honest, my escapades in the midst of those addictions are not lacking in excitement by any means. There seemed to be countless degraded situations I ended up

Chapter 10

in, and more life-and-death scenarios than I have any right to have escaped. Having said that, there were parallel parts of my life that were marked by great success.

Many people at that time would have identified me as an extreme workaholic rather than as an alcoholic or a drug addict. For me, there seemed to be a hierarchy of socially acceptable addictions, and I used work to cover the other aspects of myself that I perceived as less desirable, that is until I was unable to escape them any longer...

I have used the telling of my story for many years as a means to help others understand addiction, as well as a way to support my own recovery. And although I hugely value the healing in all directions that can happen when we have the courage to divulge our deepest secrets, especially in the world of addiction, it is not a difficult one for me to tell. The nature of addiction is to numb the things that seem intolerable, but when those more overt escapes are removed, life for some of us suffering from addiction can seem unconfrontable. And it is some of those stories that at times are the hardest to tell.

The abbreviated version of my story begins with two rounds of treatment. After being unable to stay sober on my own, I was asked to move into a halfway house, which I did only out of sheer desperation. All the ways I had punished my body over the years

The Last Place I Thought to Look

had shot my nerves. I don't know if that was the source of my seemingly relentless cravings, but for the first three or four years of my sobriety I had to put all of my energy into trying to stay clean. I remember many nights of kneeling by my bed and sliding my arm between the mattress and box springs in hopes that I wouldn't be sucked out the door into the bar down the street. I prayed. I wrote. I stuck close to recovered people. One time I even drove to a church where a priest and a nun prayed over me in hopes that some plea from an authority higher than myself would magically take the cravings away.

In hindsight, I can see that it wasn't entirely the drug and alcohol cravings I was battling, but rather something else I was mortified to admit to, and that was that I was suffering from anxiety. Oddly enough, somehow being a struggling recovering alcoholic seemed more dignified than admitting to being someone with a shaky nervous system.

My sobriety set me on a 21-year frantic search to find some way to rid myself of my anxiety. No fancy home, no perfect marriage, no amount of professional achievement, no supplement, no herb, no medication, no amount of therapy, no amount of mental and emotional understanding, and no spiritual path seemed to have the power to ward it off. I would go through periods of time when I was unable to leave my house. It reminded me of being an addict again

Chapter 10

because of the number of excuses I would have to come up with in order to hide my anxious state. But the self-loathing seemed doubly worse due to the fact that I found myself unable to do everyday life things I saw others doing without the slightest consideration, things that I myself had once done without a second thought.

Following getting clean, the good fortune I experienced for periods of time, particularly in my work, was offset by the fact that I had a secret that few knew about, that secret being that I was unable to leave my own house to make it to the nonprofit I ran for a good part of that time, unless I took a medication to calm my nerves. After 12 years and many attempts to get off of the drug, only to be in such hell that I would end up back on it, I finally reached a point where I was willing to experience the worst of all hell's in order to spare my brain and the rest of my body from any further damage. After some investigation, I discovered a clinic in Mexico that used amino acid IV's that supposedly helped people detox more easily, and that also claimed to repair the neuroreceptors that had been damaged by the drugs to begin with. It was supposed to be painless, but it proved to be anything but that. I ended up having what I would call a mild stroke, and lost my ability to move for several minutes.

In the days that followed, my ability to walk was greatly compromised and my waking hours were consumed with bracing myself against the constant threat of a seizure. Fortunately, aside from a slightly crooked smile, the outward effects of that dramatic withdrawal are not visible today. But the most intense physical, not-to-mention mental, part of my recovery following that episode took almost three years.

To recount the ups and downs of all that occurred in those 21 years of trying to find a solution to my anxiety would not only be lengthy, it would miss the point. I realize that my story of anxiety is extreme, even on the surface, but ironically it was exactly that degree of suffering that somehow also brought me back to myself. In 2007, someone suggested that I read a book by a teacher named Gangaji called *The Diamond in Your Pocket*. My experience while reading her words felt like finally returning home again after a long, winding, and arduous journey that had taken me only in circles.

My search had been almost hypnotizing in its convincing semblance of reality, but upon reading her words, "call off the search," I was, for the first time, able to see that not only had I been on a search to avoid my suffering, my whole life had been painstakingly and agonizingly devoted to it. It might seem odd to someone on the outside that I wasn't fully aware of a search that was so obviously extreme, but to me it was just like breathing. It was the way I lived my life. In most ways it seemed normal because it was the only thing I knew. My devotion to avoiding my own suffering

Chapter 10

had by far exceeded any spiritual practice I had ever committed myself to, but I had been largely blind to that fact.

That is not to say that my anxiety magically left. It didn't. In fact, to be honest, whatever undeniable shift of awareness that I experienced during my initial meeting with Gangaji seemed so utterly simple and effortless, and so contrary to the rigid way I had been perceiving my world, that I picked up and continued my search for several more months, still bent on finding "the cause" of my anxiety. But I soon found that my life was never going to be the same. Today I half-jokingly tell people that the day I first opened *The Diamond in Your Pocket* was the day I began being stalked by the truth, although I think it's safe to safe to say that the true longing to return to myself has been with me my whole life.

For all those years, if someone ever suggested to me that someday my life would no longer be defined by a state of anxiety, I would have told them that they didn't understand what it was like to be me. I was in my own prison of self-constructed victimization. With the stopping of the search came the awareness and merciful acceptance that my body is the way it is, and with that, an unmistakable kindness within myself and toward myself began to show itself. I don't typically identify with words like "stillness" or "silence," but I do relate to words such as kindness and compassion, and those are the things that I started to experience directly as I let go of the death grip I had on my own life.

So what does it look like in real life terms to call off the search? For me it has meant being released from the idea that my real life can start as soon as a particular uncomfortable aspect of it is fixed or goes away. It means that every time I find myself heading back down the habitual road of trying to work my human condition out in my head, instead of just simply experiencing it, there is now an even stronger impulse that calls me back. It is the choice to suffer or not to suffer.

Freedom has come to me in layers and with continuing and often surprising awarenesses. I have not been graced with the elusive white light experience that was secretly the goal of what I call the "spiritual workaholism" of my past. But I have been graced with sincerity and the capacity and willingness to tell the truth about myself, to myself. I have been given the choice to either turn from myself with some story of victimization or to stand up straight and tell myself the truth in the moment. And with that has also come the maturity to accept that whatever it is that needs to unfold within my own life has its own utterly reliable choreography.

Like most people, life has required me to call upon all of my resources at times, resources I sometimes was unsure I even had. And I'm grateful that I've been granted a good amount of bravery.

Chapter 10

But the courage that Gangaji speaks of is not about fighting, it's about the kind of bravery that comes from not fighting. It is about being a warrior who is willing to sit in the midst of a battlefield without reaching for a sword or a shield, even when it appears as though the enemy is rushing the gates, and that to me is freedom. It's not flashy by any means, but it was the thing that I had been waiting for my whole life. And it was in that last place I thought to look.

© 2012 Hillary Larson

After studying radio and television at the BBC in London and receiving a BA Degree in Communications, Hillary started her professional radio career producing nationally syndicated radio shows in New York. Currently, she is the producer and host of *A Conversation with Gangaji* on Gangaji radio. Every month, for thirty minutes, Hillary interviews Gangaji on a variety of subjects that reflect the possibility of finding freedom in our everyday lives, covering topics such as chronic pain, addiction, intimacy, depression, anxiety, enlightenment, death, and many others.

chapter 11

The Mystery of Our Unfolding
Zubin R. Mathai

After recently returning from India and a beautiful spiritual retreat, I reflected on how Stillness has been my only consistent companion over the years. I reflected on how Truth seems to unfold this stillness into individual lifestreams. It is a mystery how this Companion has to be revealed to have always been here, something completely ordinary, to be seen as the most precious and sacred thing in our lives.

This reflecting led me back to one of my first memories of when I was four or five. It seemed to be my first spiritual

Chapter 11

experience, but looking back now I would not call it an experience, rather something simple and effortless, a fully natural state.

I was walking across my parents' lawn to go to the neighbor's house. It was the first time my mother let me go on my own. I remember being a five-year-old boy on the front porch, but once my feet touched the lawn, something changed.

I was nothing. There was no fanfare or explosion. I was just naturally nothing. The grass was beautifully green and soft, the sun was watching over everything, and mesmerizing sparkles danced from the driveway asphalt.

For the thirty seconds it took to get to the neighbor's house, I was in a state my young mind could not explain to anyone. The best I could have done would be to answer questions about it.

If someone asked "Are you a boy or a girl?" I would answer, "That doesn't make sense here."

If they asked, "How old are you?" I would say "Ageless." if I knew that word, and as matter-of-factly as possible.

If they wondered if I was afraid, I would answer that I was fearless…and yet I was also courage-less. I would say I was neither happy nor sad for they didn't apply here.

By the time I got to the neighbor's front porch, and saw that crazy first step which almost came up to my chest, I was back to myself. I struggled up that step, climbed the rest, then asked my friend to come out and play.

The stillness I felt that day has never left. Indeed it seems to be deep within me; not my core, but after all the artificial layers are dropped, all that I am. And I see that same full, alive nothingness in everyone and everything.

I find it interesting that Truth could be tasted so young, and yet it does not always guarantee a happy or peaceful life.

What spread in my teens was a deep pool of sadness. I remember being twelve kneeling at my bed praying as my mother had taught us to do. Out of nowhere, in half-awake consciousness, invisible hands grabbed and began tightening around my neck. Behind closed eyes, I felt claws, boney, evil coldness. Now I see my young mind interpreted it as evil because there was nothing personal in those hands. They didn't care about any specifics of my story. My most precious possession at the time, the thing that craved and longed for attention, was being fully ignored.

Interestingly, I was not afraid. I was a child who couldn't watch horror movies without sleeping with the lights on for days, but I was not scared in that moment. I finished praying and got into bed. As I drifted off to sleep the silence those sinister hands placed in my mind was parted by a lone realization: my life would now change horribly. Gone would be the innocence I had, where no matter how I

Chapter 11

was made to feel alone, I still ached with a love for others. I knew I was to now live in hellish, lonely separation for a few decades.

I was bullied in school for being short, for my skin color, for being chubby and shy. I became addicted to food and packed a hundred pounds more onto my small frame. Soon I developed a severe social phobia. I couldn't be around people and when I was I just wanted to be invisible, blend into the background and disappear. I soon hoarded a passive desire to die.

There were attempts over the years, but there was little emotion around them. I didn't sob, I didn't beg for answers. I would put a bag over my head, take the bottle of pills and just wait. I would leave it up to fate. If the pills worked and I fell asleep and suffocated that would be ok. If they didn't work I would go on with life. I remember years later, when a doctor said I was pre-diabetic, feeling such a twisted blissful relief. I didn't have to do anything, just keep on eating and my body would end it for me.

So much of the sadness in those years came from vaguely feeling something in my existence was wrong. I silently wished there was more to life than just my story. I spent three decades fighting that story, trying to tame certain parts while comfortably hiding in others. I learned by example: Make the story the best you could, enjoy life, and stop complaining about it. Something in that

The Mystery of Our Unfolding

didn't feel right yet I played the game, hoping that a little more willpower, a few more tries, would find me happiness.

A very bright point amidst all that darkness was when I decided to go to India and look for a spiritual teacher. It was 1992, I was twenty-four, a university dropout with no direction and fully depressed. I was obese, patches of my hair had fallen out due to stress and malnutrition (when I moved out of my parents' house I mostly ate pizza and cake), and I had just tried another 'leave it to fate' attempt on my life.

But out of nowhere, this desire arose to go to India. How the trip came to be felt like another beautiful unfolding in this precious lifestream. The desire arose, and that itself began the unfolding, began setting in motion everything necessary to make the trip happen. I caught a beautiful glimpse of what it felt to not have to be in the driver's seat.

Nowadays, seven years after meeting my teacher Gangaji and, through her, hearing about Papaji, I sometimes wonder why I never came across him in that year I spent in India. Perhaps I wasn't ready for the simplicity of his message. Perhaps I needed to find the teacher that I did end up with over there.

After a month of ashram-hopping, no teachers, and my money running out, I ended up in the foothills of the Himalayas. It felt so good to rest after all that travel. It felt so good to take a break from

Chapter 11

the search. One day as I walked through town I saw a sad looking fence blocking off a curiously inviting patch of trees. I squeezed through a hole, walked past the noisy crows fighting over piles of garbage, past the village noises, past everything manmade until I felt completely alone. There was a boulder at the edge of the forest and river, facing those huge peaks dominating the horizon. I sat and breathed out everything on the trip so far, breathed out my life until that moment, and took everything in.

My teacher was not to be a person, but those mountains, with their gray-blue stillness topped with white shouts of snow, those gently swaying forests and those icy rivers outlining it all. What precious sacredness.

For five months my routine was the same: I awoke from the floor of a tiny, windowless room to have tea with the couple letting me stay in their storeroom, then walked to the forest to sit facing those mountains and happily raging river. I sat from morning till night, then climbed back up the mountain to the village and storeroom and slept like a baby for the next glorious day.

Back then I thought enlightenment was the goal, and the only avenue to it was meditation. I tried having a practice. Every day for weeks I would try focusing on my breathing or emptying my mind, but it was always interrupted by something. I would push that something away and try tracing my thoughts or try staring at a tree, but again that something kept mischievously interrupting.

That something crept down from the mountains, danced over the forest and sang up from the river before me. It was a playful little laughing silence. At first I didn't recognize it and thought any distraction was just me not trying hard enough. But eventually, by the end of the first month, it had whispered long enough for my attention. I gave up the idea of a practice and turned to that which had come every day to greet me.

First I saw it when I looked to the mountains. Whatever thought, no matter how involved, would get wiped away by an instant of looking at those embracing peaks. I soon started seeing that stillness in the pines, every time the wind touched them and they happily wept down a cascade of needles. Even the river, with its loudness, its waves and foaming roaming bubbles, seemed to be mouthing this silence. By the end of my time in that forest I could see that living stillness everywhere. I saw it in the back of my hands, in the little hovering bees, the smooth boulders, the village shopfronts and—when my mind and phobias didn't interfere—the faces of others.

It was a blissful time that I now feel unimaginably blessed to have been given.

Chapter 11

In the mystery that is the unfolding of truth in a life, that beautiful gift I was given in the Himalayas was sadly rejected by me. I wanted Truth to be something big, something life-changing. I expected to step out of that forest and head home a completely different person. What good was truth if it was so ordinary, so simple and pervasive? How could this energy I saw everywhere make me happy? How could I use it?

Never finding the answer to those questions, for the next fifteen years I pushed away that silence. I just wanted happiness—and not true happiness—but happiness within the story, happiness where I could still remain in control. Perhaps if I had met a teacher after my time in India they might have pointed out the final piece of the puzzle I was missing. More likely, I needed to go through those extra fifteen years of crashes of hope and disillusionment. I needed more of the story merry-go-round before seeing that final puzzle piece.

By 2000 I was living in California running a small business with my brother and sheepishly hiding behind the scenes. My life after India, after turning my back on silence, had some bright spots but also so many lows. There was another attempt on my life. There was being checked into a hospital so that I wouldn't harm myself. It was the darkest weeks of my life. But by the time I moved to California, with its sunshine and distance from my family, I had a bit more breathing room. The sadness that cursed me through my teens and twenties had slightly loosened its grasp. Even though I was still unhealthily obese and shy, and even though the emptiness of not living a life deeper than the story kept nagging me, I felt marginally better.

A few months after moving down I had another beautiful yet so ordinary spiritual experience. One night I was sitting in front of the television eating and watching a comedy show. With every funny scene I saw I laughed a bit, relaxed a bit. Then I felt a deep belly laugh and that familiar silence was noticeable behind it. The same silence I saw as a five year old, the same stillness in a Himalayan mountain or pine tree was there as the background to the laugh. And quite simply and matter-of-factly I thought I might as well stop overeating.

As simple as that.

What the story and mind couldn't win in over three decades of fighting, a simple single moment of laughter without a story did. Laughter is another beautiful facet of living stillness. It is formless and formed. It can birth anything. After a year of eating healthy I was down to a normal weight. I sometimes look back at the before and after pictures: Being my heaviest and visiting my sister and seeing my nephew for the first time, and then a year later holding my nephew after losing a hundred pounds. Dropping all that weight

Chapter 11

definitely contributed to gaining more breathing room, both physically and spiritually.

People have asked me how I lost weight; how I could give up that struggle so easily. I used to describe it as silence birthing a desire to lose weight. But now I would describe it differently. I would instead say that silence, that living, precious yet ordinary stillness that infuses everything, that everything arises and falls in, gracefully came and reclaimed the desire to choose food over Truth.

Interestingly, I can easily describe the beautiful silence that reclaimed that horrible habit. I can see and feel that precious un-laughed laughter in everything. But the mystery is how and why it came for that demon of mine, that thirty year old best friend of mine, in that particular moment.

Soon things on the surface began easing up. I made friends, had relationships, started getting back into nature and hiking. Still, a longing continued to whisper; whispered when I had nothing to do, whispered when I least expected it. But I didn't want to face it so readily. Couldn't I just enjoy my newfound normalcy?

Eventually I willingly saw that underneath it all I still wasn't happy. That, for me, took courage. It is not so easy to admit that something you fought and strived for for three decades, something that you placed all your hope in, that you pinned all the pain in your life to, wasn't bringing you the fulfillment you expected. I could now physically blend in, could be in good relationships, had the courage to volunteer for causes I believed in, but still wasn't happy. A silent drive deep within me wanted something more true.

I thought again about spirituality. I thought again about what I felt in India and if that direction held answers. I soon begged for help, in whatever form it might arrive. I begged for something, anything, to save me from the hollowing routine of thirty-nine years repeatedly crashing against rocks of hope and despair.

Shortly thereafter I came across a book by Gangaji and my life changed forever.

That book, that teaching and lineage from Ramana to Papaji to Gangaji, resonated deeper than anything I had ever encountered. With it, I finally turned to the tortured longing I avoided all my years. For the first time in this lifestream, it felt right to admit that nothing had ever fulfilled me. It felt right to divert longing directly towards Truth.

Within a month I was at my first retreat near Yosemite Park. One day, after swimming in the energy of the satsangs, of the people making up the sangha, of the giant Yosemite redwoods, I returned to my room. I decided to break the rules of the retreat and listen to some music. Through the songs, coming from that which backgrounds all, I suddenly heard myself ask a simple question: Why don't you surrender your unworthiness to me?

Chapter 11

That question, unanswerable by the story, smashed the dam holding back precious volumes of silence. And all I could do was laugh. This was different laughter, from beneath the belly, spreading and filling the room. I fell to the floor as my abdomen blissfully burst. Tears flowed and yet I could not stop the laughter. Each time I tried to, something would set it off again: the pattern on the bedspread, the silliness of a thought passing through. I laughed for perhaps 30 minutes and finally fell back to the floor exhausted.

Sometime later, on another trip to Yosemite, when I walked through the woods and felt the energy of the trees, both living and fallen, all I could see in everything was Laughter. So when I look back at that laughing fit, that huge release and opening, I can simply see that everything is Laughter playing with Love. All is that. They play together to infuse, create and reclaim everything they are. Every face of every person on this planet, whether it be showing pain or joy, is Laughter painting the canvas of Love.

With a bit of sadness at the time, I wondered why such a heart opening could not have come in the previous decades when I begged for freedom, when I ached for love from without. It is a mystery and yet is also clear. It is clear that I was resisting truth, and yet it is a mystery that Truth, which is always here, will only come when you are ready.

The Mystery of Our Unfolding

A year later at another retreat I had the courage to go on stage to speak with Gangaji. For me, for a life that wanted death rather than ever be seen by others, it was a huge hurdle. To raise my hand meant a part of me had to die, the most treasured hiding spots in my story had to be surrendered.

Once up there, Gangaji led me past nervousness, to sadness, separation and beneath that, peace. I turned to the sangha and saw that same peace in everyone. I saw that peace in their eyes, in the sunshine reaching through the windows, in the glowing carpet and walls. Everything was my heart outside my body and it infused all of creation.

I finally glimpsed the last piece of the puzzle I had missed so many years before in India. Perhaps I was not the arbitrary collection of thoughts I've roped off to call myself. Perhaps I was nothing other than the alive stillness I saw in everything.

In the seven years since I first met Gangaji I've felt the full support of this teaching and lineage. Any question or doubt I have can fall back into that support quietly blanketing everything. There are many days of sadness and impatience, there are days where I choose food over stopping, but those patterns don't hold the same power. I have seen the most precious sunrise emblazoning Grace over everything, so why, when that sunrise is always right there,

Chapter 11

would I choose to ignore it too long for the story? Why would I ever deny that even the story is shining forth that same light?

I am nothing special or different. Truth feels too ordinary to be something only for the special. When the mind is quiet I see Ramana's gentle smile in every blade of grass, Papaji's laughter in every face, and Gangaji and Eli's playfulness in every thought that arises. This lineage seems to be the first thing in my life I have fully loved on all levels. When I said yes to this teaching, it finally felt like I could relax, could let go of the steering wheel and be driven.

And I can see this beautiful depth in everyone. I see the same stillness I saw in the Himalayas and mountain pines in every face, behind every pair of eyes. Everything is made up of the same beautifully alive laughing stillness. That same peace is in every longing, every ounce of sadness. What a cruel world it would be if the answer to longing wasn't contained in everything, in every clap during a chant, in every tree, in every chair or bookshelf, in longing itself.

The unfolding of truth in my life has been a beautiful thing. When younger, it never happened how or when I wanted. Now, in my forties, when I try not to touch that unfolding, it seems perfect. My story and little life feel like a stone skipping across divine waters. With each dip into the stillness another tiny piece falls away. Each ripple spreads peace and unformed laughter across the surface

The Mystery of Our Unfolding

of me. When younger, the stone seemed to be tumbling out of control: too much spin, too much velocity. But as the life has progressed it seems the dips are getting closer together, the ripples merging to embrace more and more. I am the still, already free waters, and yet I am the skipping stone with leftover momentum. It is a beautiful mystery. It is all being taken care of.

Copyright 2013 Zubin R. Mathai

Zubin Mathai has tried his hand over the years being a software engineer, writer and entrepreneur. Now he considers himself only a quietly roaring expression of Life. Find Zubin at: www.facebook.com/zubin.mathai

chapter 12

Floored by Truth
Sutra Ray Robinson

Have you ever wondered what would happen if your mind stopped? For Sutra Ray, that experience arose spontaneously when a mental stance of absolute certainty was shattered in an instant, opening a floodgate of freedom...

It was 1975, and I was 25 years old. In all of my reading, I still had not found anything or anyone to confirm what I had been experiencing in my awareness, nor whom I felt safe enough with to share what was pouring forth from the depths of inner silence . . . except Willis.

Chapter 12

Willis was a friend of my younger brother, Kelly, and he lived two fields over from the apple orchards where I grew up in Virginia. Our families were friends. Somehow we stumbled onto each other as young adults and realized we were both having a similar experience of stepping out of the social norm and exploring what seemed like wild and amazing new ideas. We became fast spiritual friends...

We would take long walks in the orchards and wonder about the universes inside us. One day, Willis mentioned how necessary it was that we not speak to anyone of our inner explorations, saying, "Surely, they'd think we are crazy." From what I had observed, I agreed. It was, after all, 1975 in conservative Virginia. So we would sit and talk for hours in a caboose that sat just beyond my house and yard. The caboose had been a gift to my father from one of his many political admirers. It sat on its own tracks and was our special place to talk and adventure into truth.

On one particular day in the caboose, Willis and I began a long and arduous discussion about drugs. At this time I was completely against any form of serious drug experimentation, especially acid. I had no experience for this of course, but felt decisive and unwavering. I had seen and read enough to know what I was talking about. Marijuana was okay, but LSD was a whole different ball game. We talked a full 45 minutes while Willis tried to help me understand that my conclusions regarding acid were not correct. "Acid can be beneficial in some ways," he said. "It opens the mind." That might be so, I thought, but I was certain it was impossible to function on acid, and that it was dangerous in every way. I was convinced that anyone on acid would surely act odd or abnormal and would be unable to participate in society while taking it.

Patiently, Willis continued to try and explain that acid was not like that. I was adamant. I had heard all the "bad trip" stories. Finally, after trying every single angle to intervene on my judgments, he reluctantly said to me in a very calm voice, "Ray, I'm on acid right now." (Silence) I was dumbfounded, truly, and then started laughing. In an instant, my mind as I knew it collapsed in being absolutely dead wrong. Here, in front of me, was the exact opposite of my judgments and conclusions that I had collected as true and right. Willis was testimony that I had no idea what I was talking about.

In that instant of not knowing, everything shifted. My mind stopped. I was aware of a huge, flat slate board, filled with every conceivable thought, conclusion, judgment, attitude, conditioning, concept, formula, strategy, and idea that I had ever collected through reading, observing others, or from teachers, parents, or friends. Nothing was left out. Everything from birth until this exact moment was crammed onto this slate. Then, in an instant, the slate had been immaculately wiped clean. Not a trace of the past remained. It was absolutely blank. Gone. And so it was in myself. Gone!

In that moment of being absolutely dead wrong, I was floored by what is discovered when mind stops. All my conditioning had failed the test of what was actually true. It was as though the preconditioned mental circuitry had blown. The mind was not reliable as a source of absolute Truth. It had been exposed for its ignorance and limitations. When mind stops, what remains is a freshness that lies before thinking and knowing.

In that moment, life was free to be Itself—free from any past conditioning that usually preempts the present moment with ideas of past knowing. Absolutely, completely free! Whether seeing, touching, speaking, listening, singing, laughing, eating, walking, teaching, smelling, or moving, the pristine freshness of the moment was all that existed. All opinionated, defensive, protective filters of the mind, dropped away. Like a newly sprouted glacier lily in the high rocky mountain meadows that breaks through the sunlit snow on a spring day, I was hushed and floored by the exquisiteness of the present moment when nothing is attached. It was total! It was a glacier lily of the heart. The rug of knowing anything had been completely pulled out from under who I thought I was. Nothing remained.

Floored by Truth

Without any conscious effort or decision-making, a clean break had occurred from everything I had imagined to be real. Ordinary conditioned memory dropped. I saw that "Me" is what mental thinking collects and molds as identity and personality. When the mind stopped so did this supposed "me." Although mental thinking and personality continued to function, they were no longer confused with who I really am. I am that which is revealed when mind stops!

I experienced a huge, extended moment of not knowing anything. Everything I knew had been dashed in this one instant with Willis. I realized, "not knowing" was and is freedom itself! For some time to come, every blade of grass, trace of wind, sound of civilization, was filled with the core of Life—free of the collection and overlay of interpretation, judgment, opinion, denial, fear, grasping, doubt, or blame.

The predominant experience was one of amazement. I felt amazed, honored, and grateful with every single breath, step, and glance. All senses of seeing, hearing, smelling, tasting, and touching, were an extension of this core of freedom. There was not the least amount of identification linked to these experiences. They all pointed to the original awareness of God, or Goodness.

At the time, I wasn't quite sure what was happening, but I knew without a shadow of a doubt that this was Goodness beyond anything I had ever studied, seen, or been told. Its presence and

Chapter 12

simplicity completely filled my being. Goodness recognized itself everywhere. Every moment seemed to be a deeper recognition of Goodness flowing forth without any effort from this so called "me." At times it seemed as though I could not keep up with the realizations pouring through.

I was overcome with gratitude. The simplicity was silent and constant. I was humbled to the core. In that moment I realized I knew nothing, and this nothingness was joy itself...

Thoughts rebound into print,
words are stripped
to precision
and their contents penetrated.
No longer restricted,
the subtle concedes
and the source is made conscious.

© 2012 Sutra Ray Robinson

chapter 13

The Space of One Moment
Jessica Rzeszewski

On a January evening three years ago I was seated in a small, half-moon theatre in Palm Desert, California, eagerly waiting to view the movie, *Avatar,* for a second time. I was with two dear friends who had yet to see the movie. We had popcorn and soda in our laps and waited with a hundred or so people for the movie to start. The smell of buttery popcorn permeated the atmosphere. Soda sizzled its way up the straw and down my throat. The lights dimmed. The film began.

Before I tell you about my awakening, let me say that I loved seeing *Avatar* the first time, and I had returned that evening with

Chapter 13

few expectations beyond the pleasure of watching an amazing film with those I loved seated next to me. I wanted nothing more than to immerse myself in the plot once again, in the pleasing colors of humans, humanoids, and mythical creatures alike, and in the phantasmagorical landscape.

I stared at the characters on the screen, characters larger than life, and I felt connected to their thoughts and feelings as though I was on the screen alongside them. There was no separation between us. I was lying in the machine connecting Jake with his "avatar." I was Neytiri deftly climbing the massive trees in her homeland of Pandora. I was connected to those in the tribe around the Mother goddess, Eywa, as we swayed together in prayer for Grace's revival.

Three-fourths of the way through the movie, without thinking anything at all, without any back-story whatsoever, suddenly I knew, with blinding unalterable certainty that I had arrived with full consciousness into a state of non-duality. I had no idea what facilitated the movement. "Who I was" was immediately severed from "I am." I knew the moment at hand was the only moment there was. I knew that consciousness doesn't reflect, evaluate, discern, determine, or decide. It was clear to me that meaning was embedded in subterfuge; indeed, there was no meaning to anything, including "my" consciousness, which existed apart from any meaning or description I could apply to it. I knew there was nothing else I needed to do now, or for that matter, evermore.

I knew I was "the ONE" just as every other human being in the world is "the ONE," and I knew that strength of character, talent, personality, success, and failure were all created from mind, which has zero to do with being aware and awake. I knew there was no gate to walk through, although I'd wanted there to be one for so many years. In fact, my insistence that there was a gate to go through (as in every journey motif out there) had been part of the illusion.

I knew all of this in the space of one moment, one infinitesimal second, that can never, in truth, disappear, wane, lessen, or fog. I knew then that there are no lessons to life, no path, no techniques to get from one place to another, and nothing that I'd previously thought or believed or hoped for had any relevance to the moment I was experiencing.

Awake. Full consciousness. Enlightened. Except that I didn't use any of those words as descriptors. There was no need. My mind was MIA.

As the movie came to an end, I realized that what happened in the moment of birthing was actually a return to a birthright I had had all along. I was never NOT awake or enlightened, nor is anyone else, but stepping into that birthright and seeing it for what it is

Chapter 13

makes the experience feel as though a change occurs from one state to another when that isn't the case at all. Each and every one of us are enlightened; however, accepting it as so, embracing pure consciousness without filters, and recognizing our true state of being moves us to embrace our humanity and make it our reality.

I am. You are. We are ONE. It's as simple and as profound as that.

How did this spontaneous awakening occur? I can't say that I know. Before that day in the theater, so many of my life experiences were about seeking for something. After that day in the theater, the seeking ended.

In my thirteen years of searching I had explored many practices and paths. I ate as a vegetarian, performed the job of fire tender at a Lakota sweat lodge, listened to binaural beat meditation tapes, practiced urine therapy and yoga, practiced as a psychotherapist for many years, walked on burning coals half a dozen times, drummed and went on Shamanic journeys, ingested hallucinogens, and trained as a bodyworker and massage therapist.

I was a client in psychotherapy for seven years. I recapitulated for two.

I argued with a spiritual teacher for one year, followed a guru for another two, traveled to Bali to practice martial arts, bought and

The Space of One Moment

sold three houses, wrote a book, practiced meditation, hiked, and led a dream group.

I journaled about all these topics for all of the years combined, while I practiced, emoted, and processed all of the above for thirteen years.

Then I went to see a movie and woke up.

My aim while I practiced all of the above was to achieve total freedom. In the Toltec tradition, "freedom" means the attainment of perceptual fluidity, unlimited consciousness, total awareness. Not once in all of the years that I practiced that list did I term what I was pursuing "awakening" or "enlightenment." As far as I knew at the time, enlightenment was for the Buddhists and the yogis who practiced all of their lives to attain a state of being that very few achieved. Watching a movie was not the catalyst I imagined would be the trigger event for finding total freedom, but then there is no single catalyst for freedom. We *want* there to be a prescription, so that then we can simply follow it like a baker follows a cake recipe. That's what I had been looking for all those years—a recipe—a list of ingredients someone could hand to me and I could follow. I was willing to pay for that recipe and indeed I did, over and over and over again.

Performing all of those activities contributed to the belief that I was earning something I deserved. It made me think I'd found my

Chapter 13

purpose in life; that I was working really hard, struggling the best I knew how, because my belief was that life took work in order to gain something that only ever arrived in the future. Round and round I traveled with my circular rationale.

I wanted life to have a purpose, and I was willing to go after whatever it took in order to discover that purpose. What I found instead was that life is a paradox, which in many ways is a lot harder to deal with than "purpose." Purpose is logical, even linear; paradox is not. Paradox is the trickster from Shamanic cosmology. It's the experience of two different things, ideas, experiences that seem to be the opposite and, in some cases, *are* opposites, yet they co-exist. And my mind would go into paroxysms trying to hold onto those juxtapositions.

How could I be already awake as an innate condition of my humanity and yet experience a moment of awakening while watching the movie *Avatar*?

How could I work so long to attain a goal and then realize there is no "try;" there is only "BE?"

How could I follow a path for years and then realize that there is no path?

How can there be a gateless Gate?

The Space of One Moment

Paradox throws us into performance, into problem solving and perturbation. Paradox is difficult to experience, to write about, to grapple with, and at the same time paradox became the anvil upon which I hammered out my process.

A few weeks after my opening at the theater, I came down with a cough, a cough that wouldn't let up and turned into a painful hacking that pummeled my ribs and put everything on my calendar at a standstill. I went to the ER and was diagnosed with pneumonia.

At home I lie in bed without moving between fits of excruciating coughing. The coughing was painful beyond anything I'd ever experienced. The antibiotics made me nauseous. While lying there, I began to view the pneumonia from a different perspective than the usual "I have pneumonia, I'm now on medication, and I'll get better soon." Instead, I lay there whispering, "What's going on here?" How had I become so painfully ill in such a short period of time? Never before had I been healthy and suddenly fallen ill with such vengeance.

I began to look at the event through an energetic lens and took up a conversation with my lungs. I went online to research the Chinese 5-Element Theory to find out what my lungs could possibly be communicating to me and found out that the lungs belong in the element metal, are yin in nature, and deal with grieving.

Chapter 13

Grieving resonated with me. In a nine-month time period I'd been fired from my job, sold my dream house, and was an observer to my daughter's breakup with the father of my three-year-old granddaughter. What an agonizing year it had been!

I began to view the pneumonia as "stuck energy," and I was building up a case for doing something to consciously allow the grieving to move through me. The urge to rid myself of the intensity of the pain was as intense as the pain itself. "Move on through and be done with it!" I wanted to scream. "Quickly!" But my lungs spoke to me and indicated that *they* were doing the grieving; it was nothing my mind needed to control or become a surrogate to. The illness wasn't stuck energy; it was energy expression at its most potent. I thanked my lungs for doing such a powerful job of grieving, but there was another surprise element to the grieving I hadn't seen coming.

It turned out that the grieving had as much to do with the tremendous loss of "the journey" as it had the loss of a job, a home, and a family member. My journey—everything included in the list above—had been taking place for nearly fifteen years. Now, the continuation of those events would no longer be necessary.

In addition, the discovery that I could feel pain as a form of expression without labeling it "illness" was profoundly powerful. I no longer felt the need to "do" anything beyond allowing the pain to do the job it had come to do—and to stay out of its way while the job was executed! I experienced the pain in direct proportion to how much value I'd placed on the journey. Now, the hacking cough, the sore ribs, and the nausea were the visceral avenue for feeling grief and loss. As my lungs paid tribute to my loss, the grieving was released, and I was able to let it all go.

The remainder of that first year after awakening continued to bring to light different ways of viewing the world and my place in it.

I became aware of nature in a very different manner than I had previous to awakening. I recognized that the trees weren't begging to be flowers; the ocean wasn't looking forward to evaporating into the sky; my ears weren't bargaining with my nose to switch senses; my bones hadn't rebelled because they weren't blood molecules flowing through my veins; the snails weren't swapping with the cows for a higher position on the food chain.

Nope. Everyone in nature was at peace with who and what it was. No striving. No competition. No success. No failure. Just being. Being *what is* from the moment of its inception.

I became aware that my thoughts and feelings had not been "white washed" as a result of the awakening. I was annoyed at times. I experienced communication snafus with loved ones. I instigated goals to achieve as a means of "doing." All of these ways of being were ghost limbs, chronic ways of being in the world that

Chapter 13

didn't just disappear that night in the theater. My assumption had been that after enlightenment I would be "perfect"—never ruffled, always serenely cool and collected, ever ready with a sage response.

I became aware that my "condition" was irreversible. Not once have I doubted or questioned what happened to me while watching the movie *Avatar*. At times, in speaking with people about awakening, I see that *they* wonder about my awakening, and I realize how difficult an experience it is to describe and to articulate. My words may be confounding or lack clarity, but "I am" is clear and grounded in knowing.

In a nutshell, here is my current experience on a daily basis.

Nothing dominates. A better way to say it might be that "No-thing dominates." Both are true. The positive and negative space that defines life is equal. My emotions, moods, beliefs, experiences, and events are all on the same plane. One doesn't take back seat to the other. What occurs each day is center stage, and I engage everything that occurs with equal fervor.

Events that occur on a daily basis no longer "hang around" like they used to. I experience what happens each day and then it's gone. Past and future are anomalies.

I have less of a sense of "lack" as in disappointment or frustration. I have a sense of satisfaction and peace with what occurs. What occurs each day is what is and not a shadow of what it could be based on my desires or demands for what I want to take place.

I feel a greater sense of spontaneity because my days are less burdened with expectations and assumptions. Previous to awakening my expectations and assumptions acted as ballast that prevented me from rising above them.

I feel less driven therefore more present for everything as it occurs.

Because of all of the above, I'm more open for non-patterned things to occur. From that very non-patterning, curiosity and creativity are evoked. I see that my curiosity and creativity are innate ways of being in the world whereas before awakening they occurred less consistently and less spontaneously.

I'm aware of the flow of events as they occur around me as though they have a "responsibility" to me rather than the other way around—as though my place in the flow is better balanced than it used to be. Events meet me as often as I meet them. Subjectivity and objectivity switch places fluidly and aren't locked into a dual perspective.

I have a feeling of…I want to say confidence, but that's not it…it's more a feeling of certainty, of constancy, that events in my life will *unfold* in a manner that will support what I've said above. It's not merely the expectation that "only good things will occur," but it's a feeling that whatever happens, I will take it in stride as though that event and me are partners, co-conspirators in my individual, yet universal and collective, existence.

© 2013 Jessica Rzeszewski

_____

Jessica is a Licensed Marriage and Family Therapist (MFT) working with military families in Hawaii. She can be contacted at: eyetoenlightenment@gmail.com

chapter 14

Forgiveness: Key to Peace, Gateway to Openness
Kia Scherr

What do you do when the worst thing that could possibly happen, does happen? This is what happened to Kia Scherr, when she lost her husband and daughter in the 2008 terrorist attacks in Mumbai. Through her courage to open to this horrific loss, the course of her life was forever changed. In this writing she shares the revelation of her inherent oneness, even with terrorists, that brought her back to peace when her life was shattered into pieces and peace seemed impossible.

Chapter 14

In November of 2008 my husband, Alan, and my 13-year-old daughter, Naomi, traveled to Mumbai for a modern meditation retreat at the Oberoi Hotel. In June of 2008, Alan had made the trip to Mumbai to scout out locations for this retreat, and was about to make a deal with the President Hotel, when the Oberoi matched the same group rate at the last minute. Being a much better location on Marine Drive, naturally he signed the deal with the Oberoi.

In July of 2008, David Headley, a Pakistani American who was working for a terrorist group, was scouting locations for an attack that would take place in November. As he was waiting for a movie at the Inox theatre in Nariman Point, he wandered into the lobby of the Oberoi Hotel, adding that location to his target list. On November 14th I said goodbye to Alan and Naomi at the Dulles Airport in Virginia. Little did I know this would be the last time I would see them. We kept in touch through email and phone calls over the next week and on November 24th I had my last conversation with my husband and daughter. Naomi had just gotten her nose pierced and had sent photos through email. She was so excited as I shared the news that her test scores had come in for her entrance examination to a top girls boarding school in New York. She had scored 95% overall and the news filled her with joy. Alan and I excitedly discussed all of this and our last words to each other were, "I love you."

Forgiveness: Key to Peace, Gateway to Openness

The next day I got on a plane to Tampa, Florida to visit my parents, sons, brothers, and sister for our Thanksgiving holiday. When I checked my email the following day, (November 26) there were no messages from Alan or Naomi. Later that afternoon, as my mother and I were getting ready to watch Oprah Winfrey on TV, the phone rang. It was the managing director of Synchronicity Foundation, where Alan was vice president, which was sponsoring the modern meditation retreat in Mumbai. She told me to turn on the news right away because the Oberoi Hotel was being attacked by terrorists. I dropped the phone in disbelief as my family came running in asking what was happening. For the next two days we watched in horror as the terror attack in Mumbai went on and on and on. We had no idea where Alan and Naomi were and prayed that they were safe in their rooms. Friends and family called, joined our prayers, and called upon their friends to pray with us.

Because Alan and Naomi were unaccounted for, my eldest son Aaron sent their photos to CNN in case they were unconscious somewhere in Mumbai with no identification on them. E-mails of more prayers began pouring in from all over the world. We felt comforted by this loving support from so-called strangers. It was Friday, November 28th when I got a call at 6 a.m. from the U.S. Consulate in Mumbai, confirming that they had both been shot and killed in the Tiffen Restaurant at the Oberoi Hotel.

Chapter 14

For the next few hours my family and I sat together on the living room sofa, numb and in shock. As we watched the aftermath on CNN we saw that there was one lone surviving terrorist. As I looked at his photo on the TV screen, the words of Jesus Christ came to me: "Father, forgive them, they know not what they do." I then said to my family, "we must forgive them." At that moment I felt a ray of peace enter my heart, and I knew that this was the right thing to do. I knew that if I could forgive the terrorists, I could go on living and give forth of myself in love. In those moments, I had no idea how I would do that, but I knew that forgiveness was essential. "There is already enough hate," I told them. "We must send our love and compassion."

As I shared this experience with Master Charles Cannon, spiritual director of Synchronicity Foundation, who had survived the attack while trapped in his room for 48 hours, he said, "Yes, this is a message to be shared. We must open to a greater vision to create positive outcome to this tragedy." I agreed to join him in this endeavor and over the next few months One Life Alliance was born.

The primary message of One Life Alliance is to honor the oneness and sacredness of life in ourselves and in each other. Our mission is to engage in this conversation with educators, students, businesses, and governments around the world, and to implement projects that put this message into action. This will increase the peace index in individuals, communities, and eventually, all nations. As Persian poet Saadi wrote: "Human beings come from the same source. We are one family."

I have learned that forgiveness requires a deep level of acceptance of what has occurred. This does not mean agreement with, or any kind of pardoning or condoning of the action that hurt us. It simply means acceptance of the reality of the situation and letting go of the incident, which cannot be changed. Once we accept, we can move forward to heal and continue loving no matter what. This acceptance brought me to an inner peace that cannot be shattered because in that peace is contained the essence of humanity. I am that essence. I am me, and I am you, and we are one. It is choice I make every day.

Forgiveness allows me to keep my heart open. Un-forgiveness keeps me shut down and contracted inside. Holding on to anger, hatred, and feelings of revenge will poison us and keep us locked in a prison of darkness. Forgiveness lets in the light of love, compassion, and peace. By choosing forgiveness on a daily basis, we unlock the prison doors and transform our lives as love flows into every interaction and every moment of solitude.

This is true transformation. When we transform our lives, we transform everything around us. There is a still a world of possibility, even when the worst thing happens that could possibly

Chapter 14

happen. I invite you to stay open to the possibility of peace, love, and compassion through the power of forgiveness. Our survival as a human race depends on it.

© 2013 Kia Scherr

Kia Scherr is co-founder and president of One Life Alliance, a global peace initiative that is bringing tools of peace to education, business, and government, beginning in the United States, India, and Mexico. She may be reached at kiascherr@onelifealliance.org and www.onelifealliance.org. In 2011, Kia published the book *One Life Alliance Pledge: 30 Days to Honor the Sacredness of Life.*

chapter 15

LOVE of My Life
Elizabeth Schmidt-Pabst

There are many moments I could share about being with my beloved and beautiful spiritual teacher, Mariananda, and the radical effect that being her student has had on my life. But I suppose it's easiest to just start at the beginning.

When I first began coming to Satsang, long before I was a member of the Blue Planet Sangha, (the sangha that has gathered around Mariananda), I remember sitting in Satsang, looking at and listening to Mariananda, and not understanding a thing. I tried so hard with my mind to understand and could grasp nothing, only a big fat headache. While my head was busy trying to understand

Chapter 15

what can only truly be heard in the heart, a process had begun deep inside me. Looking back, I would compare myself to a glass of muddy water.

Being near Mariananda's presence of unconditional love was like pouring clean clear water into this glass. It brought all the mud in my glass to the surface, and I can tell you there was a lot of mud! And who knows what dried up muddy layers have yet to surface! As Mariananda always reminds us, "Always be a beginner!"

At the time I did not know what was happening, but I was drawn to her and Satsang like a moth to a flame. I remember little of my first Satsangs, other than that I cried through my first year of attending them. I cried and I cried, and I sweated like crazy. I sometimes even brought a spare T-shirt with me. I cried and sweated and was aware of a horrific feeling of shame within me. It was extremely uncomfortable in many ways, but a love, before unknown to me, had touched my heart, and it compelled me to return again and again.

I was so moved by her presence of love and truth, it reminded me that there is something deeply true in me, something until then I was not even really sure existed. But it resonated within like the ringing of a bell, and this ringing was louder than all of the skepticism, fear, and doubt the mind could conjure up. For the first time in my life, I had the feeling that someone was seeing me, seeing me deeply, seeing who I really am, and this knowing cut through all doubts directly to my heart, giving me the sense of "HOME." I did not know what, where, how, or why, but the sense was unshakably there: HERE is HOME.

Now, more than ten years later, I have discovered that it is not only finally being seen that set my heart aflame, but that it goes even deeper. It is the *seeing itself.* I could see love, joy, endless compassion and truth in the eyes and presence of my teacher, a living human being before me. I had never seen that in someone before. Not from my parents, not from any partner, not from anyone I had ever met. Mariananda says you can only see that which you, yourself, are inside. So, this seeing and being seen meant for the deeply troubled person who I was, that there is indeed hope. That love and joy and compassion must be even within someone as messed up as I was. That was the biggest surprise for me.

As far as worldly worth is concerned, I had been a screw up. At the time, I was a single mom and lousy at the job. I was a college drop-out, I was depressed, and I was obsessed more with the search for a boyfriend than anything else. I was in constant war with my ex-husband, and I believed I was very special, possibly even enlightened. Actually, I was just a hippy with a lot of experience with drugs and well-traveled. I was living on welfare because I felt I was better than just going to work somewhere. Inside, I was

Chapter 15

disappointed and I believed that love and truth and joy were actually just silly ideas left over from childhood. It was totally life changing for me to see that true love and truth are in fact real, being lived by a real living person, and that everyone (including me!) is eternally welcome to discover it.

Sometime during the first months of attending Satsang with Mariananda, I went to the front to ask her a question. I did not really *go* to the front, I did not plan it, and I certainly did not know it was going to happen until it was. But I remember my heart carrying my legs to the front, and that as I walked there was no turning back. So often I had sat in Satsang with some question in me, something I would never ask out loud, because I would never endanger my self-image by speaking up and possibly humiliating myself. Even then, my un-asked questions were always answered in Satsang. Mariananda heard and answered all questions of the heart, spoken or unspoken. But there I was, with my heart carrying me to the front to sit face-to-face with this person unlike anyone I had ever met before. I believe my first question was how to find an anchor, something to hold on to, but more than these few words, I did not speak and I saw later on videotape that the dialogue I had experienced and the answers I had received to my many burning questions, came without me having to ask them out loud. Mariananda saw right through me, she heard every question and was equally as surprised as I was that I had not actually spoken them out loud. I had never experienced this with anyone other than through drugs in my teens, and there I was not making a sound while she read every question from my heart.

I knew then and there: "This is my teacher, my beloved, profoundly devoted Sufi Master, the one I have been searching for I knew I had found her: the LOVE of my life. The following years of spiritual work brought up a lot of darkness that still was inside me, much that needed cleaning, clearing, looking at, and letting go of. The mud covering my heart was at times very contradictory to this great love of all loves, making me at times a very stubborn student. Again and again, caught in the (as Mariananda puts it quoting Chris de Burgh) "classical dilemma between the head and the heart." But my heart was touched, a fire was lit, and no matter how deep I sometimes found myself in the illusion of the ego, I could no longer run away. Running, which had been my second nature until then, was just over.

Now, when I sit with Mariananda and others from the Blue Planet sangha at her sacred "around the kitchen table Satsang," I notice how still my mind has become. How the turmoil and debris of the muddy waters has been filtered, transformed, and cleansed just by being near her. I do not know how this works, but I experience it every time I am near her. A stillness arises, and a peace spreads out within.

Chapter 15

This peace has spread into all areas of my daily life. Before I met Mariananda, I had so many problems. Like I said, I was lousy at being a mom for my son. It took me years to admit that. I remember the burden that dropped when I laid my head down on Mariananda's kitchen table and finally gave up trying to be someone I was not. I had to admit to myself, "Yes, I really am a bad mother." At that moment, things began to change! I never thought that acceptance alone could change anything, although I had seen how fighting, striving, and trying created only more suffering, exhaustion, and resignation. Without Mariananda, I would never have believed that acceptance and forgiveness really have the power to change my life.

Today I have a normal relationship as a normal mom with my normal son. Everything is within the wonderful 'normal madness' of raising a child, and it is grounded in the love and trust that came out of finally admitting what a mess everything was. It came from finally accepting my human imperfection without finding a parent or God to blame.

Through Mariananda I could see through my very "new age" ideas of what earning money was all about. Mariananda taught me that the outer life has to be enough in order so that I can be free to turn inward. I went back to school, became a nurse for palliative care, and am now so grateful to have been blessed with a job where I can serve others by coordinating hospice volunteers who guide the dying on their last journey. Every day I thank God for being enabled to serve in this way. For five years now I have also been lucky enough to have found my life's partner in my best friend. After years of searching for love and only finding sex, I found a man who did not run away when I said the words, "I am in a spiritual group and have a spiritual teacher," a man who really loves me even though and maybe because he knows me. A partner with whom I can cry, love, and laugh. I was lucky enough to find the partner of my life within the Sangha.

But the greatest proof for me that true down-to-earth nitty-gritty spiritual work has changed my life is my relationship with my ex-husband. He is my barometer for my own ego. If we have troubles, I know I am headed in the wrong direction. We have had peace for a long time now. Real peace and healing took place in a relationship where there was only fighting, competition, bitterness, distrust, and anger. For me this is such a huge miracle. My whole messed up life has become a wonderful life inside and out. Even in the midst of difficulties, life has become a blessing. In the past year I hurt my back terribly while moving a patient. The months that followed were of great physical pain and the inability to sit or even walk more than a few steps. Even through all of this, the peace and acceptance that I have learned through Mariananda carried me through it all,

Chapter 15

making me honestly grateful even for that experience, excluding nothing, really learning to say yes to all that arises inner or outer!

I have found Mariananda to be living love and vigilance in every moment, in every situation, no matter what. This is so radical and so different from what I thought the "spiritual life" would be like! In truth it is doing the very dirty laundry, the stuff hidden way in the bottom of the laundry basket, washing it again and again to find there are still some stains, and again and again until eventually I'm doing it with a smile. This is the amazing invitation that my teacher continually offers me. To always, always be a beginner, no matter what came before, however great or horrible the experience or ego-driven drama that preceded this moment, right now. Over many years of rigorous and ruthless deep inner work guided by Mariananda, I have been lucky enough, again and again, to experience moments of true freedom. My life has become a constant rediscovery of that freedom who I really am, and I am so grateful to see that freedom mirrored back to me now in my day-to-day life.

In deep gratitude and love for my beloved teacher, Mariananda.

© 2013 Elizabeth Schmidt-Pabst

chapter 16

what is this?

Miriam Louisa Simons

*So blatantly in my face
yet unable to be seen?
Closer than my breath
yet unable to be reached?
Shining through the mind
yet unable to be known?*

It's taken me a lifetime to understand that my personal motivation on the spiritual journey was a bit unusual. I wasn't looking for an antidote to suffering—not at the outset anyway. I

Chapter 16

wasn't trying to escape anything. I didn't feel incomplete. I was a happy if ingenuous kind of person.

But in the lottery of life I was over-endowed with innate curiosity. As a child I was a question mark on small feet—and I assumed everyone else was, as well. In fact, my childhood assumption was that the content of all human brains was identical to my own. I still remember the shock (I was about ten years old) of realizing that I was definitely 'different' from my brothers and school friends. That was my tardy moment of individuation, the drop-kick into separation. The birth of dear wee Queen Me.

I was also born with the 'wonder' switch turned on—the one that makes you wide-eyed with wonderment at the miracles of life. (Later I came to understand curiosity and wonderment to be a natural pair.) It seemed to me that the greatest wonder was that life happened at all. How come it was so blithely taken for granted? How come no one seemed to pay heed to this miracle? How come it was never in the news except when it arrived as a newborn or departed someone's body at death?

> Miraculous: supernatural; surprising: L miraculum
> from mirari: wonder; F mirus: wonderful
> — Oxford Concise Dictionary

Looking back, it seems my journey has been about penetrating the nature of this "miraculousness" and the odd way its presence

what is this?

seems to cause me to disappear. An important part of that journey has been my passion for making things. From early childhood I loved making things because it was during playful immersion in creativity that the miraculous would often manifest. The word "art" wouldn't come into it until much later, when there was an artist self up and running. Then, I would notice that the miraculousness would only come to play in the artist's absence. But that's another story.

There's another thing I must mention, and honor, about my birth: I arrived just before the eve of my mother's birthday and, as a pair of pint-sized blue-eyed Aquarians, we were joined at the hip. Lifetime buddies, sisters, soul-mates, which was incredibly lucky for me, because my Mum was wide awake as to her true identity. She never missed an opportunity to remind any of her offspring when they were immersed in some story about themselves: "But that's not who you are, dear one!"

In retrospect I realize that as a youngster there was no question as to what the 'I' was. It was *unbounded spacious knowing*. I wouldn't have had access to that vocabulary, but I do remember the sense of headlessness and the absence of solid boundaries to my body. (This caused a few ownership problems with my brothers!) Even after the arrival of individuation this experience remained constant—although preoccupation with the stories that were

Chapter 16

accreting around my teenage self slowly began to dominate my attention, heralding the beginning of The Great Forgetting.

In spite of having morphed from a mischievous gawky kid with big teeth and a too-high forehead into a sweet sexy thing with a gung ho hunger for experience, I avoided the perils young women often fall prey to and headed off to University and Teachers' College eager to find answers to my questions. I thrived on Literature, Philosophy, and especially Phenomenology of Religion.

It was as though I was following a thread back through the archives of all that had been written about life's big questions in an effort to make sense of that "unbounded spacious knowing"—the all and everything of my early experience. So, rather than the "What am I?" question, I was well and truly led by the nose by the "What is this?" question. *What is this aliveness living me? What knows this world? What is this mind-silencing mystery?*

Around this time—my late teens, I guess—I began serious spiritual scrap-booking. I called these books my *x-files*. (x-plore, x-cavate, x-periment, x-tend…) Amazingly, fifty years later, I still have many of them, and marvel at the wisdom that was being scribbled between their covers by that young woman. She was also cutting and pasting quotes from sages and scientists—anyone who was addressing her question. There were drawings too, and photographs of life's miracles: usually close-up details of color,

what is this?

texture and form—the early indications of her preferred visual language as an artist.

To be able to look back down decades and recognize that this child and young adult knew so intimately and instinctually what the sages have pointed towards for millennia, is extraordinary. In my ingenuity at the time, I assumed that this was the case for everyone, until a close friend assured me that it wasn't so, and that "Most people don't even *think* of the kinds of questions you come up with!"

Obviously I had to find people who did. It meant leaving behind my homeland and family. Along the way there were experiments with being a freelance fashion designer, a wife, a globe-wanderer, a serious meditator, a yogini, an artist, a teacher, and on occasion, all at the same time. It's remarkable the way my questions mapped out the journey and ensured I never stagnated in any backwater for too long.

In the mid-seventies teachers like D T Suzuki, Chogyam Trungpa, Krishnamurti, Guru Maharaji and Rajneesh (Osho) were delivering Eastern philosophy to the West, opening our outer and inner eyes. I took to meditation like a duck to water and received initiations and instructions left right and centre. A real spiritual junkie. If cosmic visions, divine light, celestial sounds, and the humming dynamo of the Word had been enough for me, I'd

Chapter 16

probably have stopped there, grinning goofily. But they weren't. They were entertaining but ephemeral; it was the changeless *knowing* of these phenomena that interested me.

One wild meditation ride is worth mentioning, however, because it demonstrates the tricky business of staying on-task when there are so many psychic temptations for the seeker. During a meditation in Christchurch, New Zealand, an earthquake struck, and it wasn't in the earth's skeleton, it was in my own. The spinal column. Ice, fire, and blinding light. I was one of a group who were meditating with a visiting Indian swami, and in a private interview I later confessed that the amazing light, vibration, and sensory explosions I'd experienced didn't mean that much to me, because they had come and gone, like everything else in experience. What I really wanted to know was this: *What is it that is aware of these phenomena without ever changing?* He wobbled his head and smiled. "That," he said, "is the Mother of all questions. Only you can find out—by yourself and for yourself!"

Right. How helpful was that?

Some years later, I came upon the writings of J Krishnamurti. As a teacher I found his books on education of great interest. However, it was his personal writing in his journal, *Krishnamurti's Notebook*, that thrilled me to the core. I recognized that here was someone who was totally intimate with "unbounded spacious knowing." Not only that, but his book *The Impossible Question* cut to the quick of my own life-question, sending me to my room for days of mind-melting. I set off to meet other souls who were exploring his ideas.

Krishnamurti insisted that people *look for themselves*, inquiring deeply into their actual experience to see if "something sacred, timeless, and incorruptible" actually existed. Yet the tendency to conceptualize the possibility and allow it only to "special" sages was tenacious. The reality of our shared essence as pure silent knowingness was overshadowed by the endless exploration of *what it is that acts to overshadow*. In the habitual inquiry into what blocks creativity, co-operation, harmony, and the natural flowering of a happy life, the immeasurable Silence from which these effortlessly arise was largely neglected.

For me personally, it was a painful lesson. The felt presence of that Silence, that spacious unknowable knowingness, became vague. My heart grew heavier and my life more confused. I had tumbled into a conceptual chasm, along with just about everyone I knew. And the odd thing was that we all meekly accepted that such was our lot as "ordinary" beings.

Yet it would be impossible to overestimate the importance of those years of dialogue and inquiry with others similarly drawn to Krishnamurti's teaching; and working with the extraordinary

Chapter 16

students at the Krishnamurti schools worldwide was by far the highlight of my career as an educator in art and design. Formal and informal dialogues with David Bohm, with his profound understanding of the creative mind, slowly verified my suspicions: habit-driven thinking and the movement of genuine creativity are incompatible. And since the presence of the "miraculous" in the art studio and in my life was clearly when genuine creativity happened, I began to glimpse the relationship between spacious silent knowingness and manifestation.

Meanwhile, Queen Me had grown up and was performing as a very complex ego-self. Even after the true dynamic of thinking was intellectually appreciated, and the self was understood to be "just another thought," it was a thought that still had a death-grip on my tail. In retrospect I see the perfection of this, and the part played by that illusion, but at the time I was mostly at the mercy of its mechanisms, acting out the common and cringe-worthy symptoms of delusion. And since you can't have delusion without suffering, I got an honorary degree in that too. Yet, alongside, underneath, and throughout it all, the "unbounded spacious knowing" was inescapably present and utterly unaffected. And, I knew it. In spite of the split, I knew it. It was a kind of schizophrenic dichotomy that would take radical circumstances to resolve. And on-cue, life provided them.

what is this?

Fast forward to the new millennium and I'm in Queensland, Australia. It's Easter, 2002. If you could peek through the window of my small sanctuary this is what you'd see:

A small, weary, middle-aged woman sits on a zafu. She is crippled by an old injury that will soon require surgery. She is thousands of miles from her work, her colleagues, her friends, and her sangha. Her brilliant life seems reduced to ashes.

She is withdrawn but not sorrowful for she accepts her circumstances, and she deeply loves the two sweet friends—her parents—she has crossed the world to care for in their ancient age.

She has inquired deeply into life's mysteries and questions. She has been blessed to be taught and mentored by great souls. The zafu is her friend.

She stops—perforce. She sits. She stays. This time there is no escape.

Bereft of all the notions of who she took herself to be, how her life should be, how the world should be, and how she should fix it all, there was space, silence, and stillness.

The spacious silence and stillness was something she recognized. She'd known it intimately as a small girl, and it had never left her for a moment as she journeyed through the days of her life. She had spent her entire life gathering information and

Chapter 16

verification about this "state-that-can't-be-experienced." But now life had turned her towards it by cutting off all means of physical or intellectual escape. Life itself forced a free-fall into an "unbounded spacious knowing" so catastrophic that nothing remained of the illusory separate self that had appeared all those decades ago and been queen of its tea party ever since.

* * *

It never occurred to me that there had been any kind of spiritual "awakening," because the free-fall was entirely at odds with my beliefs about such an occurrence: I didn't fall into bliss or love or glorious feelings of grace. Yet the unforgettable moment marked a mind-shift, and it was clear there'd be no going back because it heralded a new way of being in relationship with the world; a way that to me was actually very old and very familiar.

To coin an analogy, I felt like a penny that had been free-falling through a slot machine for some time, and even though the final tumble happened instantaneously and spontaneously, there had been stages where the penny had landed on a level and spun or wobbled for some time. I can identify three such stages:

Stage one: the penny had fallen hard onto an existential plateau when I realized that nothing could be proven to have any existence *apart* from the sensorial technologies in the body/brain of a sentient creature. That was a pretty big OMG moment.

what is this?

Stage two: it wobbled around there awhile before toppling further when I failed to find evidence of anything other than the functions of consciousness, anywhere. Whoa!

Stage three: it fell clear through the works with the logical conclusion that my own existence, and likewise the existence of all "others"—indeed, the entire field of my experience—could, therefore, be nothing but a dream-like arising in consciousness. Boom!

These three notions had been orbiting my brain for many years, understood at some intellectual level. However, being a bit dense, I had failed to see the connection between what they explained about the world, and the "spacious knowing" in which that world arises. The pernicious penny had remained safely in the purse.

My new circumstances had delivered me to the banks of the Rubicon. There'd been difficult times, times that challenged everything I thought I'd understood. Ripeness must have been ready. A huge letting-go of the old *me-mine-myself* story was called for, and it happened without intention or volition on my part. It was a spontaneous surrender.

When the penny fell clear through, it took the bottom of my gut with it. I felt like throwing up. The top of my head seemed to lift off. I struggled onto my feet and said to myself (among other

Chapter 16

unprintable expletives): *Well then, old girl, that's it! No one at home. No one to beat up. And no one to wake up! Haaaaa!*

First there was a kind of numbness and shock, a feeling of disorientation, of falling into an inner vortex, and then, an opening out into unbelievably serene spaciousness. Oceanic.

No sense of a center, no opacity, no separation.

Unbounded spacious knowing. Again.

* * *

It felt as though a cyclone had torn through the memory-matrix called "me," sweeping away the loose trash completely and reorganizing the rest so that perception operated from a new perspective. It bears repeating that it had nothing to do with any effort on my part.

An entity is defined as "a thing that has real existence." In spite of my lifetime intimacy with "unbounded spacious knowing," I had believed that I was a "real" entity. Doesn't everyone?

But to be a "thing," an object needs a subject to recognize it as a "thing." If I'm an object with real existence, what's the subject that is recognizing "me"? If I turn around to examine this subject, I immediately find that it has turned into another object being observed and recognized by the same subject! If this lunacy stops, what happens?

what is this?

If I stay still, not moving into lightning-fast conceptualization, if I watch that notion called "myself" with its bag of beliefs that make it seem solid and separate in time and space, it reveals itself to be, simply, another (miraculous) conceptual object.

The indisputable "aha" for me, was—and is—the re-cognition that only spacious knowingness is ever *actually experienced*, and that it "does its thing" effortlessly without the presence of, or necessity for, an *independent experiencer-entity*. Sense-ing, observe-ing, perceive-ing, recognize-ing, are ceaselessly *function-ing* from and as unbounded spacious knowingness. The headless kid with no body-boundaries had known the score from day one…

I wasn't one of those (mythical?) creatures whose "aha" moment sees them dissolve into instant bliss and love and live happily ever after, but I was ok with that. Over the decades I had learned to stay with the truth—the "what-is"—of my experience. Something trusted the process completely, and the evidence thus far had indicated it was probably a lifelong one.

I had fallen out of my mind into the unbounded spacious knowingness that was so familiar. So simple! So simple that it had taken a while for my adult mind to accept its all-inclusive nature. I had been schooled to believe I would find something I could identify with—something that would be the ultimate and enlightened "me." What a hoodwink!

Chapter 16

With "Queen Me" in its right place at last—off the ego pedestal and back into the toolbox to be useful as and when needed by life as it acted out its agenda—there was now unlimited room for everything archived within this body and mind to turn up and be transformed. Transformed? From contraction to release. From resistance to acceptance. From agony to agape. It was horrific to realize that the archeology of stories invented over a lifetime to protect Queen Me was a seemingly bottomless pit. It wasn't fun, but I was blessed with the help of a couple of awesome angels in this process. *Grace.*

One of these was a silent sage who brought me face-to-face with the reality of the fierce Grace that bestows sanity, health, and the priceless predisposition of curiosity. *Humility. Compassion.* The other was a Lama who guided me on a six-week silent Dzochen retreat, giving me back my original question and ruthlessly revealing all that was conceptual about my understanding. His parting instructions to me: "Keep emptying!" *Gratitude.*

And so it goes. Nearly seventy years worth of shadows to acknowledge and release, rather than box-and-bury; rivers of tears to shed, welling up without invitation or cue, but always bearing a revelation of contrition, forgiveness, or gratitude to be embraced.

So how would I describe myself now? As ocean and drop, wave and particle, nothing and something, life and death. I feel like a tidal breath-being, emptying and filling for no rational reason.

what is this?

How extraordinary to discover that *the more emptying, the more fulfillment*—which is only logical really, since the "boundless spacious knowing" cannot be separated from the world it knows. (Holy moly: that includes darling Queen Me, happily hosting her tea parties in the toolbox!)

The writing in those *x-files* decades ago marked the beginning of a journey that had unfolded graciously (but certainly not painlessly!) without any help from me. The circle had traced its circumference—from the innocent knowingness of the newborn, to the realized knowingness of the Unborn.

The Unborn? Just another label for that unknowable miracle, *élan vital,* growing every heart, and beating it to its own unique rhythm.

* * *

Post script: a memory surfaces. When Mum and I were celebrating our 70th and 40th birthdays, respectively, I recall asking her a question as I looked at her soft wrinkled skin and silver hair: "Mum, what does it feel like inside a seventy-year old body?" Her blue eyes twinkled as she replied, "Exactly the way it felt as a seven and a seventeen year-old! Ordinary. Sweet. Innocent."

Yes. Exactly.

Chapter 16

© 2013 Miriam Louisa Simons

Born in New Zealand, Miriam Louisa Simons has lived in Australia since moving there from Europe to care for her frail-aged parents at the end of 1999. The "Day" she mentions in this essay occurred in 2002. Notes she kept during the year following the "free-fall" are retrospectively published on her blog at www.echoesfrom-emptiness.com. After the death of her mother, she began another blog and dedicated it to her mother and her own favorite topic: the unborn light of awareness. It can be found at www.this-unlitlight.com. Expressing from her passion for the arts and creativity, Miriam also founded and edits the website and blog: www.theawakenedeye.com. Her studio practice finds its cyber home at www.wonderingmindstudio.com. She continues to cradle her lifetime question. Sharing pointers with others in an informal context is an increasing delight. Please feel free to contact her via the blogs, or on Facebook.

chapter 17

Never Forgotten

Unmani

As a child I always knew who I really was. I always knew that I am not limited to or located in this body. And as much as I was confused and lost for many years, I never really forgot this knowing.

When I was a child, there was only this. Life happening. Not-knowing. Innocence. I always knew this. Nothing ever happened. I saw the joke. I saw others pretending. Then fear arose and with it a sense of "me in here" and "them out there." What is expected of me? Must I play their game? I don't want to. I don't know how to. What is this crazy world where everyone is pretending to be a someone?'

Chapter 17

Confusion. Trying to fit in. Trying to survive. As I became a teenager, confusion turned to rage. I was burning with rage against the pretense. I was angry with the world. There was a feeling of something terribly, terribly wrong, something missing.

When I was with my parents in the garden, my Mum or Dad would often say, "Look, isn't that tree beautiful?" I would often answer with a kind of angry "Mmph." "There are not some bits that are more special or more beautiful than other bits," I would think, *They are all in me. They are all of equal value—the dirt under my fingernails and the blossoms on the tree. The trees, the flowers, and everything in the play of Life is my home. Of course it is all amazingly beautiful, but this beauty is not an idea.*

People used to say things like, "Wasn't that great, yesterday?" and again I would feel cheated and confused. The past had never happened. I didn't know how they could believe that it was real. All words seemed to be such a pretense. When other children at school asked each other questions, such as, "What is your favorite color?" I didn't know where to find the answer. I had no identity that I could refer to. What I really knew beyond the world was not being reflected back or acknowledged in the world. I didn't know how to live this game of being someone. I doubted what I really knew and thought that there must be something wrong with me.

Never Forgotten

I innocently tried to play being someone in order to survive in the world, but I felt more and more confused and heartbroken. I tried on different identities to see if they would fit. I tried to find the ideal relationship or career, and I even thought that by analyzing and working out the patterns of the thoughts with a psychologist, that I would "work it all out." I was searching for the missing link. That piece of the puzzle that would fill the emptiness and make the pain go away.

When I was 17, I left England and ended up spending the next 20 years living in various other countries. I was continually searching for the right identity that would fill the emptiness that I assumed was wrong with me. I learnt so much from everywhere I went, but one of the most significant places that I lived was in India for three years at the Osho ashram in Pune. And although Osho was no longer living, I fell in love with his words and his message of freedom. Meditation was new for me and I loved it. I loved the dancing meditation, and I danced for hours every day. I loved the respect for silence. I had never come across that before. I took the vow of *Sannyas,* and I received a new name from the women whom Osho had left in charge. I was given the name Unmani, which in Sanskrit means "no mind" or "beyond the mind." I have kept this name as well as my birth name, Liza, because I like how this name carries no identity or history and is simply a strange sounding word.

Chapter 17

I don't feel like Unmani or Liza is who I am, but when I hear the name Unmani, I find it especially amusing.

Although I loved Osho, I still felt that I was searching for some kind of rest in myself. I was quite unhappy and felt that nothing that I did really went to the root of what I was looking for. I decided to do a primal therapy group where for five days we regressed back to childhood to reconnect with our inner child and to express what we never had a chance to express to our parents. During a heavy catharsis session, I broke my ankle by attempting to kill my mother as I punched and kicked the mattresses and padded walls. I was so fired up and desperately depressed that I didn't care about the pain. I continued to jump and dance on my broken leg until I was taken to hospital. I managed to have my leg put in plaster and then come back to the last day of the group. As I sat in a wheelchair and listened to the therapist say, "This has been just a taste of the work that you need to do on yourselves," my world went black. I felt so angry. *It can't be this way,* I thought. *It can't just be an endless search. I know it's not.*

Because of my broken foot, I spent most of the next month lying in bed staring up at the ceiling. I felt so lost and so at the end of my strength. The pain in my heart was physically and emotionally unbearable.

Never Forgotten

I had heard about a woman called Dolano who was a Zen master giving satsang. I had never heard about "satsang" or "awakening" before. When I first heard this term "awakening," I had no idea what it meant, and I was not really interested in finding out. It seemed like yet another spiritual experience or goal to be chased after. I already knew that these spiritual goals had nothing to do with actual fulfillment. But when I heard that Dolano was only inviting people to come to her who were ready to die, I had a deep sense that this was for me. So, in my pretty suicidal state, I went to see her.

At first I didn't realize that what she was describing was what I had always known, because I couldn't believe that someone was actually speaking it out loud. But then after a couple days of hearing her, it hit me that for the first time someone was acknowledging what I had known since I was a child, that there is no identity, that there is no answer, and that there is no need to know the answers. There was such a laughter and relief. This is what everyone else is searching for. What a joke! I was so grateful that someone had the courage to speak the real truth so that I could hear it.

After this, a great relief was felt but there was sometimes doubt and still the questions of how to integrate this into my life? What do I do with this now? What about all the old conditioning and

Chapter 17

emotions? How to deal with them? I spent two more years dabbling in various other spiritual teachings and enquiring deeper into the beliefs I had gathered about who I thought I was supposed to be.

One night after a disagreement with a friend, I spent all night trying to figure out the difference between arrogance and humility, until something deeply relaxed in me. I recognized that everything is happening *in me.* Absolute arrogance and absolute humility— there is no difference. All the words, concepts, doubts, confusion, fears, conditioning, and more, is all happening in me. None of it ever means anything *about* me, because it is all appearing *in* me. In that moment, the search was over, but there has been a continuous unraveling of old beliefs, and an endless free-fall into not knowing how to live as someone in this game of life.

When we are children, when we are new to this life, all we know is openness, innocence, a sense that anything and everything is possible. We are empty of ideas about how things should be. There is simply a not knowing and an emptiness waiting to be filled. There is just a curiosity and wonder at whatever is here, a sense of being at home and no fear of losing anything. Everything is welcome and enough. There are no restrictions or boundaries. Pure love. Pure being.

But at some point we learn that being in the world isn't supposed to be that easy. According to everyone else we are supposed to know who or what we are. We are supposed to know what we want or where we are going. We are supposed to abide by the rules of our family and fit in with society. We have to quickly learn how to be a person in this crazy world. We have to learn that there are limits and boundaries of what is socially acceptable or not. We have to learn to contain our energy. We have to learn to restrict what we say or do. We begin to learn that we have to play the game in order to survive in this world.

After a while we learn the rules of survival so well that we begin to believe them ourselves. We begin to believe that the limits of our thinking or what other people have told us must be true. Everyone else in this wondrous existence seems to believe that they are separate individuals, and most people appear to know how to be one and what that even means. People seem to have ideas about how things should be and seem to know the rules of the game.

When I was a child, I remember feeling very lost and alone amongst these strange adults who had strange rules. I found what they said and did often very contradictory, and also often such a contrast to what I felt beyond all the words or actions. I learnt that my inner knowing was not supported or confirmed in the world. It was something to keep quiet and buried deeply inside, as it only seemed to cause trouble. Adults would say one thing and mean something else. They would do something and I could feel that their

Chapter 17

heart wasn't really in it. They were doing it to fit in because they thought that it was something they should do. There seemed to be a general fear of really letting go and trusting that sense of clarity and openness beyond all the ideas. When I did state what seemed to me to be the most obvious, it provoked defensive reactions, denials, and seemed to cause a lot of pain. So like everyone else around me, I learnt to keep quiet about what was really going on.

I watched people pretend to be someone with an important life story and a meaningful existence. A lot of people seem to be struggling to find, and then to hold on to, some meaning in it all. People search for meaning and fulfillment in their work, in their relationships, in what they possess and in their achievements. But much to their continual dismay, whatever meaning they find, they eventually realize it is only temporary and then the search for meaning goes on. There is never a sense of being truly satisfied. We are always imagining that satisfaction and the final rest will be just around the corner. But it never is.

Some people start searching for meaning and fulfillment through spirituality. At first this can seem to offer great worth and meaning, as it seems to be beyond the mundane and ordinary daily life. But at some point spirituality starts to become another false identity. It can make you feel like you are more special because you are a good meditator or energy healer. It is about chasing temporary experiences of bliss and running from uncomfortable experiences that you are forever trying to fix.

At some point it is about recognizing the fact that any meaning is only a temporary belief, and any fulfillment is only a temporary experience. Nothing in this play of experience is permanent and there is no final rest to be found in it. In being deeply honest about what you really know, or in fact don't know, the simple truth is so obvious and always has been. I am not what thought says I am. I am watching it all happen. I am aware of every experience. I am awareness itself. That is who I really am. I am aware of the thoughts, but not affected by them, and I am also watching this woman called Unmani who is living a life. She is in me. She is an expression of life itself, which experiences itself like this. She is an instrument to feel and express life energy.

Thought cannot do or understand this truth. It is too obvious and simple, and thought loves to complicate everything. There is no practice that can help because there is nothing that is needed or lacking. You are already everything that you long to become. Once you see that you are not your thinking, then you can see more and more that all the thoughts only serve you. They are not the enemy, as we usually believe. They are only trying to help. They offer practical suggestions, they try to solve problems, and they try to protect you from all kinds of threats (real or imaginary). In seeing

Chapter 17

the thinking for what it really is, life isn't taken so seriously and this person living a life is freed up to be just as she is. She blossoms more and more, and there is a falling in love with her more and more.

Knowing that I am not limited to this seeming individual, Unmani, means that she is free to be limited. I am aware of her, and I am her. I feel everything that she feels. I experience everything that she experiences. Paradoxically, who I really am is untouched by any of it, and yet at the same time I am so touched that it brings tears of gratitude for this play of experience. This paradox cannot and does not make sense. It is not about maintaining some kind of distance from the personal reactions, it's not about never feeling uncomfortable, and it is not about holding on to a particular experience of being aware and untouched. Nothing is required in order to be what I am. And in the falling in love with this person, I know I am absolute clarity, absolute strength, absolute love, absolutely everything. I am every experience, and it is all happening in me. Everything that appears to be outside is inside. My true nature is absolute emptiness, which is filled with all of this.

Nothing has changed since I was a child. But I have gone on a journey of pretending and hiding, and have come full circle back to the beginning, only now with the maturity of an adult who can acknowledge, appreciate and courageously feel and express who I really am in this play of experience. There is no end to this unraveling and falling in love with myself in everything and everyone. It is only the nature of thought that longs for a final resting place in this never ending, moving, changing, wild and sensual life. But if there was an end, then it would be fixed and stagnant. Who I am is life itself, and that is never limited to what we think. It is always an unraveling mystery.

© 2013 Unmani Liza Hyde

Unmani is originally from the UK, but has lived a nomadic life in many countries around the world from the age of 18. She has had no "home base" for years, and travels around the world holding meetings and intensives relying on the generosity of people who have been touched by her message. Amazing people in so many countries have helped, supported, and hosted Unmani over the years. She lives in gratitude to those who are willing to open their homes and their hearts to freedom. She is the author of *Die to Love* and *I Am Life Itself*, both books of satsang.

chapter 18

Enlightenment is Not an Experience
Enza Vita

I prefer not to dwell on the past because it has nothing to do with the essential message of this story. And that central message is that enlightenment is not an experience.

Whatever experiences we may come across in our spiritual journeys, we are not any of those experiences, but rather the one who is witnessing them, the pure awareness cognizing them without thought.

The experience may be of bliss, of silence, even of nothingness, but it is not what we are. We are the experiencing of it.

Chapter 18

We must leave all experiences behind, and keep going to the point where every object goes—silence, bliss, nothingness—and there is nothing left but our own subjectivity. Then, no bliss is more blissful than that, no silence deeper, no nothingness truer.

As the story goes...

It was the last day of a meditation retreat, and for a few days I had been unable to sleep as a familiar wave of energy ran up and down my body. It felt as if I was plugged in to an immense source of energy. Even though I was functioning on very little sleep, I awakened that morning feeling good.

The bell rang, announcing the first meditation session of the day. I sat on a chair at the back of the meditation hall and took a deep breath in and out. I let myself relax into the cushion while being careful to maintain an alert presence.

Over the previous few months I had been working at maintaining a balance between relaxation and 360-degree openness all around, while at the same time being alertly aware. Too much relaxation and I would fall asleep; too much alertness and I would become agitated.

After a few minutes into the session, a huge rush of energy began rising within the centre of my body. The feeling was so incredibly powerful it frightened me. My gut reaction was to open my eyes, and I looked toward the meditation teacher. I could recognize her facial features, but I had to focus hard to keep her face from floating away. I closed my eyes again, trying to settle with the energy that was now shaking my body. Then a thought floated by in consciousness: "What is perceiving this?"

Eyes still closed, I sensed a movement arising from a vast bottomless chasm, and as I began to focus my attention on it, it appeared as though I was looking into a reflective surface.

A shiver of terror went down my spine as I realized that what I was seeing was actually myself moving. Not the self I was familiar with, but something so infinitely vast, totally unexpected, infinitely unimaginable, and so utterly terrifying that my mind gave up. I disappeared into a nothingness with no-thing in it. No forms, no sounds, no thoughts, and no self—just absolute nothingness.

The next thing I was aware of was the bell signaling the end of the sitting meditation and the beginning of the walking meditation. I found it difficult to comprehend anything. I couldn't remember my name or who I was. I got up and went outside. The world appeared different. The trees shimmered vibrantly in iridescent hues. Everything was extremely clear and had a sense of immediacy. Every little thing was alive and present. At this point, I laughed, overtaken by joy.

Chapter 18

My joy turned to awe as I began to sense a breathtaking *presence*. It was incredibly vast, bright, and alive, but also personal, intimate, and intense, radiating pure love everywhere. It was *harmonious*. It was *infinite*. It was *unimaginable*. It was *perfect*.

Another meditator approached and asked me about a salad she was preparing. Without any effort, the answer rolled off my tongue. To my surprise, she didn't notice anything different about me. To her I still appeared to be a normal and coherent woman, even though I still could not recall my own name.

I found this so funny, I had to keep myself from laughing out aloud. I didn't feel ready to give a reason for my sudden bout of laughter, because I was not sure she would understand.

Gradually the experience subsided and by nightfall, I was back to normal reality again, back in name and identification.

In my bed that night, I reflected on my experience. While I felt indescribable gratitude for it, I sensed that the experience I'd just had was not complete. If it had ended, it could not have been the "real thing." I knew that there was still something that I wasn't fully seeing.

Since I was a child, I had had many spiritual experiences like this, and they all had a beginning, a middle, and an end. They were always about "me" having "my" experience. I intuitively knew that what I was looking for was not only before and beyond time and space, but also before and beyond any ideas of self.

Effortless Fruit

The next day I woke up feeling very sick, and for a month I lay in bed too weak to move. Then, as suddenly as it had come, the sickness left and I decided to go out for a bit of fresh air.

I was walking down the street when suddenly I realized I was not existing in the individual shell that had once encased my personality so tightly. The person I'd once thought of as me, rigidly held together and kept separate from other individual existences, had melted into something indescribable, an infinite space containing everything and giving rise to everything.

I was that space, I was everything in it, and I was the awareness of it, yet the space and what appeared within the space were not "two." Since there was no line to distinguish between "my" awareness and the images I saw, I realized that this experience was not happening to a personal self. Both appearances were simply *in* and *of* awareness, and whatever perceived this was awareness *itself*.

Everything appeared very normal, very ordinary, and yet something was different. I was not *having* thoughts; I was what *contained* the thoughts. The same was true for *all* appearances, including emotions, states, sensations, and experiences. Everything

Chapter 18

was appearing and disappearing within the space that I am. There were no boundaries or borders.

I was everywhere and everything—the mid-afternoon sky, the sound of my boots hitting the footpath, and the chewing gum sticking to them. I was every blade of grass, every tree, and every leaf on that tree. I was every bird that flew across the sky, every slab of concrete I walked on, and the rubbish bin waiting to be collected. I was also the body-mind called Enza—all of it—body, sensations, feelings, and thoughts. As Enza I was walking in the sun, basking in it, but I was also the sun offering light to everything and bathing itself.

I saw that this awareness had always been here. Right here, in my ordinary life, I had always been this, and this "me" included not only infinite space but also everything in the past, everything in the future, and all of time. Amazingly, I had never before noticed it, because by searching for the magnificent and the exciting, I had continuously overlooked it.

What, then, was left? Just the flow of life, as it appeared, without the overlay of "states." States were still experienced, but only as within this wholeness, as an aspect of wholeness.

Unknown Grace

Enlightenment is Not an Experience

At first I avoided speaking about this to anyone, having decided that I was not going to share my "experience." At the time it seemed better to keep quiet, partly because I believed I would not be able to fully communicate it, and partly because the history of the entity I had believed to be me, was one of not wanting to do anything that made her overly visible.

If I were to start talking about this, it was bound to happen that others would project their notions onto me. I knew that I may be met with skepticism, and that some would question my intentions, that I was doing it for the money or the fame, or that I wanted to be a guru.

But slowly, as the stronghold on this mind-generated identity started to loosen its grip, I became more willing to do whatever life wanted of me, including the writing of a book if it could help others to recognize their true nature as that which is always and already, completely and naturally FREE.

© 2013 Enza Vita

Enza Vita, publisher and editor of *Woman Spirit, Health and Wellbeing,* and *Innerself* newspaper, is the author of her soon to be released book *Always Already Free – What is Enlightenment and*

Chapter 18

What Does It Matter Anyway? from which this article was extracted. For more information about Enza or to contact her, visit her website at: www.enzavita.com

chapter 19

A Christmas Gift

Alison Walker

From being a very small child I have felt passionate about discovering the truth of "who am I." One of my earliest memories is of being six years old and gazing at the dark inky black sky, with stars twinkling in a majestic, incomprehensible spaciousness, and feeling overwhelmed. I was aware that stars had been here millions of years, so I asked myself, what is the point of this little life?

From then on a search for answers was my passion. I began exploring churches, and later I explored other religions. As I was an unhappy, lonely child at boarding school, I prayed a great deal and sometimes found solace in a small sanctuary at the top of the school

Chapter 19

buildings. Here, as I prayed for help, I felt what I then called Jesus answer my prayers. These prayers were simply calling for help in my loneliness and the answers came as peace. At one time as a teenager, I thought I was being called to be a Nun, but when I prayed about it, my answer was, "No, not again!"

As I left this stage of my life behind, I left religion. I held God responsible for all the unhappiness of my life. At eighteen, I felt that I would be better in charge! I thought that life would be easier that way, and I began to explore the answers to who I was by marrying and having children. Later, as a family therapist, I explored other avenues I hoped would give me a better story. However, I found that the old question, "who am I?" would not let me go.

Eventually I realized that my hope of doing better without God had failed. I began to meditate and walk quietly in the countryside. I explored complimentary medicine and then healing. I became involved in healing and meditation and found I had this extraordinarily close contact with an elderly Indian man who appeared in my meditations. He talked to me of many wise and wonderful things. He was teaching me about unconditional love.

After my husband retired early from his profession, I felt guided to move with him to Scotland, and together we started a little meditation center where I taught meditation and ran awareness

A Christmas Gift

groups. By this time our son and daughter were both married and in their mid-twenties, our daughter living in London and our son in the Midlands. Neither showed any interest in what my husband and I were doing. In fact I think they found many of the things somewhat imaginary, especially our views on the rapidly changing natural world. They were about their own journeys and anything that challenged that was far too uncomfortable. I suspect they found me rather mad!

And so it was on one Christmas, when I discovered something so precious, it felt like a Christmas gift that would last forever, and it came through huge suffering.

My daughter and her husband came to visit us in Scotland. They had not been married long and were living in London. Scotland seemed a long way for them to come. When they left we felt all was well. However, this was the last contact we were to have with them for two years. My daughter communicated that she did not want any contact and that we were to leave her alone. She offered no explanation.

For the first few weeks, I tried contacting her many times in an effort to understand. She refused, however, to answer the phone or letters. It was devastating for me. I had felt close to our daughter, but my husband had had a quite difficult relationship with her, and so seemed less hurt and upset. I simply did not understand what had

Chapter 19

brought about this breakdown in our relationship. It felt respectful to leave her alone for a time and meet her request for no contact.

I was on a very conscious spiritual path at that time, with many beliefs. Maybe I shared those beliefs too enthusiastically. I was aware of huge changes in the world and felt the need to be a part of raising awareness and encouraging others too. I was practicing meditation and running a meditation group, so there was a good deal of meditation going on to help with the pain. I always had the "hope" or expectation of understanding and clarity that would lead the situation into reconciliation. I wanted an outcome that was "my" best outcome. I chanted and visualized good healing outcomes and beautiful peaceful scenes. I prayed and affirmed good things continually and sought healing for all sorts of bodily pains. I walked in nature to try to find peace, but the endless dialogue in my mind went on and on: "What did I do or what can I do or how have I failed?" I distracted with social meetings in an attempt to avoid my deep pain and despair I felt about the loss of this precious personal relationship with my daughter. I believed that if I just tried hard enough, I could bring about an outcome that I wanted. I found it so frightening to have no control. And I also found it hard to talk to anyone about the pain I was in. There was so much shame and a deep sense of failure as a parent and a teacher of meditation.

A Christmas Gift

This pattern of behavior went on for two years, through which time I was suffering a very great deal both bodily and emotionally. I felt isolated and lonely. By the second Christmas I was desperate enough to try to ring her again on Christmas Eve. My husband pleaded with me not to try, wishing to avoid seeing the pain of my possible heartbreak. Again, I rang with no response. This time, spontaneously, my heart broke. It just happened. It was a shattering experience. My heart was broken open with grief and pain. Nothing to do and nowhere to go but just to open to the heartbreaking pain. I collapsed into my breaking heart and cried and cried, finally falling asleep.

When I woke up on Christmas Day I found myself in total bliss. I realized how deeply connected I was to everyone and every living form of life, silently, without doing anything. I knew with certainty that love was here and everywhere always, and that I am love. I became totally aware that in all our diversity we are all one living expression of love and life and this love needs no confirmation...it needs nothing at all! All is well and is always well. There was awareness of many lives with many different daughters and mothers. I seemed to know that these lives were about learning through direct experience. Clarity came with the awareness to live and let live.

The night before, as I had cried myself to sleep, I had heard my old guide telling me, "well done, well done, well done." I had no

Chapter 19

idea what this meant, as to me crumpling and collapsing felt like total failure. I believed I should have been strong and not weak. Yet having learned from my guide over the years that true love was unconditional, here I was finally discovering it for myself, which was something very different from belief or learning. It seemed as if the old shell of myself had disintegrated, and I was now connected to something extraordinary.

This enfolding love brought the freedom and the clarity of knowing that my daughter was about her own life in her own way. If love is here and we are both love, there is no need to "do" anything but to lovingly let go. With this all-encompassing love present, it was easy. I needed nothing and no special outcome. I could be myself! Life, having pushed me to open, was finally gifting me with a willingness to surrender. I could do none other. Finally, I *wanted* to let go, and I experienced the bliss of total relaxation and surrender. How this bliss had really come about, I had no idea. It seemed a complete mystery. Yet here was Grace offering me joy in the middle of heartbreak. It felt extraordinary that only the night before a crucifying agony had been present, and then the next morning an experience of sublime bliss. All I knew was that out of failure had come this total certainty that I am love and that failure is loved too. This failure cracked open my heart and broke up the story that I had let consume me. In pain, I had found truth. In the darkest place, I had I found this amazing light!

A Christmas Gift

I had spent a lifetime controlling painful feelings, and there had been many painful episodes in my life. As a child I had learned to control my feelings to survive. I had learned to try to be a peacemaker in a very dysfunctional family. Yet on that Christmas night when I lost all control, what was revealed was an extraordinary peace that held everything. There was a clarity that nothing had gone wrong and all was well. All that had ever stood between love and me was fear.

As a child, the ability I had to see myself and witness myself had often felt confusing. It had caused me to feel unsure of who I was. Yet in that night of the deepest heartbreak, in that traumatic yet extraordinary time of bliss, again I was able to witness this suffering self and at the same time see the peace that is always here. I now know that awareness was showing me that the body is a vessel for learning and opportunity, but that conscious awareness is truly who I am. I may be living an experience of mother, wife, friend, and so on, but under it all is this love that I am.

That Christmas Day was a gifting beyond measure. It was filled with ecstasy and joy. It seemed as though beauty and light touched everyone and everything. Outside, it had snowed and crystallized, so there was silence and peace in the land and in my heart. My heart overflowed with joy and laughter. Some part of me knew what this

Chapter 19

pain had gifted me, that love can appear as a kiss or a kick, and this allowed me to have confidence in life itself as the teacher.

Sometime after this revelation, my daughter rang and there was reconciliation without questions or the need to peddle a story. I realized that if I needed to know what had happened, in time I would. Slowly and tenderly, we resumed our relationship in the Now, and bit-by-bit I came to learn that what had gone on had to do with the story of my daughter's own pain and shame.

The Christmas bliss continued to fill my life for about three months, then gradually it disappeared. Having had no real idea how it had come or where it had gone, it was only later that I realized that at some level letting go had been part of it. However, I still was not seeing my patterns of addiction to suffering. As the overflowing joy slowly subsided, I found myself back in pain and confusion, searching even more deeply for some kind of fulfillment that would last.

My husband and I decided to move to New Zealand, and although NZ was stunning and life was good, there were still no really satisfying answers. Once again, total despair set in. Finally, I prayed for help, and the result of that prayer was a book coming my way by the name of *The Diamond in Your Pocket,* authored by a spiritual teacher named Gangaji. I had never before heard of Gangaji, but that book changed the direction of my search. It

A Christmas Gift

changed this life! I finally stopped looking for answers outside myself.

It was only after meeting Gangaji that I was able to uncover a lifelong pattern of avoiding or controlling pain. I had made war with anything that I had judged as unacceptable. In an attempt to manage life's hard and difficult lessons, I had been searching for spiritual strategies that would help me manage pain by rationalizing it and attempting to understand it. Slowly I became aware, through Gangaji's support, that when I choose to open and surrender to pain and fear, instead of avoiding it with a multitude of strategies and beliefs, I can discover once again the Christmas Gift. That the truth of who I am *is* this joy, peace, and love that is always here under all situations regardless of season. I am it and so too are all loved ones and all of life's expressions. We are one.

I have come to see that pain is a part of life, but suffering is a choice. I can choose to accept pain, or I can fight it and try to control it in a huge variety of strategies and stories, practicing anything in the "hope" of a particular outcome. That is a sure way to suffer!

What is so beautiful is that pain or discomfort has become a friend. Not that I like the feeling, but whenever I allow it space, it inevitably leads me home. So does any other feeling that I do not like. Life leads me to discover what is underneath feelings, when I

Chapter 19

just receive rather than reject or control. Thanks to Gangaji I realize that attaching to stories is a cover for trying to manage discomforts, pains, and fears. Yet with willingness and courage I can choose to open to life as a gift, whatever it looks like, because under all stories of difficult circumstances is this love that is the ground of all life! Under all stories of "my life," I discovered the truth of myself and found freedom! Even in an Earthquake, there are huge gifts, which I have written about in a book.

The season of New Zealand earthquakes that began in September, 2010 and are still continuing today with over 11,000 on record. For me, the experience of the ongoing shaking brought up story after story of avoidance and control. Addictive patterns can be very tenacious! I find that every difficult story is really covering a feeling I have deemed unacceptable. I know now I have a choice to go back to old patterns or to receive life. Slowly, I see the choice. Nothing means anything unless I attach to some story about others or myself, and now I know I am not the story!

Now I also know how this precious Christmas gift came and where it seemingly "went" and where it can always be found. Sometimes I find myself laughing out loud at the joy of the on-going discovery of this love that is always here. Yes, it is present in all circumstances, and yes, this is who I am! All Life is a gift and I am deeply grateful for being pointed the way home and for the

A Christmas Gift

persistent pain that pushed me to awaken and open to freedom. Life will go on with all its ups and downs, horrors and joys, but knowing the truth allows life to be received as a flow.

© 2013 Alison Walker

Originally from the UK, Alison Walker currently lives in Adelaide, South Australia, near her daughter and her daughter's family. She can be reached at: walkerutd@hotmail.com. Alison's recent book, *Blogging Awake: Self Inquiry through 10,000 Earth Quakes,* was a finalist in the NZ Ashton Wyllie Book Awards. In a year of horrific earthquakes in Christchurch, New Zealand, the book is a day-to-day account of self-inquiry into, "Who am I?"

chapter 20

The Way of Tenderness

Zenju Earthlyn Manuel

Gently Meeting All That Is Difficult

When my teacher gave me the Dharma name Ekai Zenju, which means "wisdom ocean, complete tenderness," I could not swim in the ocean, and I was especially not tender with a liberated sense of life, but tender, or rather sore, in the way of feeling wounded by life. I was hardened by the violence against me as a young child and the poverty in which my migrant Louisiana parents had to struggle in raising three daughters in the wilds of Los Angeles. As a child, I was hurt upon discovering that others saw my dark body as not beautiful. As I aged, I was afraid of being annihilated for making

Chapter 20

love with others regardless of gender. In essence, I was bound to feelings of injustice, rage, and resentment. I held my life tight in my chest, making my body ache with pain for many years.

Depression, unhealthy relationships, dependency on substances such as food, alcohol, and drugs, and thoughts of suicide were responses to the tensions between what I felt was imposed upon me and the true nature of life in all of its beauty and perfection. So, you may ask how is it that a two-spirited[1] woman of African descent, who has experienced deep internal and external hatred, become "Zenju," complete tenderness?

Some teachers suggested: "Just drop the labels and you will be free." Some advised: "You are delusional. There is no self." But these flat, simplified, diluted excerpts of vast teachings were not the words that shook me from my pain. In fact such guidance felt to come from voices that sought to further *their* idea of harmony, or those who were uneasy with difference and required an instant elimination of it. I wanted to shout, "I am not invisible!"

Recently, while participating in a silent seven-day retreat, I began to practice leaving everything. Leaving my aspirations, hopes, dreams, identity, all notions of being this or that, of doing this and the other. I was to say goodbye to these things for seven days. I sat for hours simply breathing in and out. As things came up, I would say goodbye, bowing dutiful at the parade of passing thoughts.

The Way of Tenderness

During one of the hours, my deceased mother came to mind. It was if she had come to sit silently with me. I could not tell her to leave. I began to cry immediately. I couldn't tell in the moment the reason for the tears, but I could feel an upsurge of old pain from the times my mother would beat me in her rage. How could I be tender? I kept breathing and crying with this vision of my mother. Her face was sweet and she was smiling. She was not appearing as the rageful person that had frightened me at a young age.

I opened my eyes to wipe the water that had been held between my eyelids. I looked around the room and realized that I had separated from everyone in the room for that moment. With the wounds between my mother and I so present, I could see how it had kept me from fully engaging with folks my entire life. I could be kind to others but I was not tender. I was afraid to be soft and allow others completely into my heart. I cried more as the room seemed to darken and I fused in with the darkness. We were all in the dark. In the darkness, I was a part of everyone and everything whether I accepted it or not. I was invisible as was everyone else in the room. "*I am invisible*," I whispered to myself. As I continued to breathe, I felt a warm breeze near my face, yet there were no windows or doors open and it was cold and raining outside. I thought perhaps it was the spirit of my mother. And then I said no, perhaps this is how tenderness feels when it arrives.

Chapter 20

When I turned towards the hurt in the silence, I entered the way of tenderness. I began tilling the hard ground of life into the soft soil of healing. I sunk deep into the soft ground beyond the beautiful appearance of a two-spirited woman of African descent to a place where the source of life was revealed wordless, nameless, without form, completely indescribable...completely tender.

As I eased below the surface of being a two-spirited woman of African descent, I needed to be gentle. If I were going to go past such a beautiful floral exterior of my life, how would I survive the namelessness? I felt lost, and at the same time fear and caution were attempting to shut down this experience of unhooking my heart from mistreatment and discrimination, from disregard, from hurt, and from the separation I had experienced and accepted as my life. The unhooking squeezed my chest, restricting the blood flow in my neck. It felt as though I was having a heart attack.

The namelessness required breathing. I could not be in the vastness without inhaling and exhaling, and so I breathed hard and deep for some time. Eventually, I was escorted to the emergency room to see if in fact I was having a heart attack. The way of tenderness almost wiped me out. And perhaps it does wipe "you" out.

Most of my life I participated in the political, sociological, and psychological analysis often used in dealing with mending the gap between harmony and difference in our society. The "isms" began crowding my mind, bursting intellectual brain cells and causing an internal battle, because I fell into almost every marginal group one could conjure. The experts seemed harsh and biased in dealing with racism, homophobia, classism, ableism, ageism, or any situation that would oppress one group of living beings based on erroneous ideas of superiority and inferiority. There was no "correctness" that could sustain "correctness" over decades. None of the trainings or paths meant to end the suffering of oppression seemed to transform suffering at its core. So the way of tenderness, without effort, had presented itself to me in a Dharma name and a road toward liberation from the woundings of life.

Yet this way of tenderness is not a behavior, philosophy of life, or a conceptual view of life. It is not a solidified path but rather an unfolding experience of life as I live and breathe.

How could I be gentle *and* angry? How could I meet disrespect or disregard with tenderness? How can I be gentle when there is war?

I say how can I *not* be gentle *because* there is war? Gentle does not equal quiet. It does not mean I will not be fully human and angry when mistreated. It does not give acceptance for anything or anyone to hurt or abuse life. It doesn't erase the inequities we face in our relative and tangible world. The tenderness that arose in my

Chapter 20

life went beyond and was there to meet me and assist in a liberated and well-hearted engagement with life rather than sinking into pain and separation.

The way of tenderness [my own definition] is the path of a gentle response to discord or clash. It is a response that is below the surface of what appears to us when we are seeing, hearing, touching, smelling, tasting, and thinking. It is a response beyond the mind and body. It rises up with the willingness to not know the reason for the tears, with the willingness to be taught like a newborn baby about life.

The gentle or tender response does not come in manipulative words or passivity. You cannot be trained or taught to walk this path by any teacher at any cost. It cannot be practiced.

The way of tenderness I speak of appears on its own. It comes when the doings of your life have rendered you silent in the corner, and there is nothing you can do but sit in the distress. The path may present itself when the rage is so palpable that you gag. It may come as a lion's roar, and to charge at the lion would be deadly.

The way of tenderness comes despite the fear of *not* fighting for our lives. The path arrives even if there is an inability to sink below the appearance of things, including our identity and aspirations. We only need to unfold our arms so that we can breathe through the fear of our ever-present harmonious nature.

The Way of Tenderness

[1] two-spirited: A Native American perspective of what many call gay or lesbian. I prefer it because it includes spirit and not just political ideology.

© 2013 Zenju Earthlyn Manuel

Dr. Zenju Earthlyn Manuel, author, diviner, visual artist, drummer, and ordained Zen Buddhist priest, was born in Los Angeles, California, to parents who migrated from Creole Louisiana. She is the author of the *Black Angel Cards: 36 Oracle Cards and Messages,* and *Tell Me Something About Buddhism* with foreword by Thich Nhat Hanh. She can be reached at: www.zenjuearthlyn-manuel.com

The Journey Home: Discover Heaven on Earth
Volume 1 — 2012

This is the story of the road to nowhere, a journey of the heart. Like many facets of the same diamond, we are the collective ONE; each with a sacred story to share of our journey on this road called Life. Life is not who you are, but rather an experience pointing you back toward who you are.

www.IntheGardenPublishing.com

BODHI UniversiTree
Holistic Online Learning Center!

Bodhi UniversiTree invites you to explore our Universe based on a more holistic approach, merging the left (science) and right (spirituality) hemispheres of the brain for a deeper, more mature understanding of God/Creation, who you are, and why you exist.

www.BodhiUniversiTree.com

one
THEMAGAZINE

ONE is a quarterly online magazine bringing the good news of awakening from around the world. Featured are deeply personal accounts of non-dual realization and newsworthy events that exemplify and celebrate our true nature as ONE.

www.OnetheMagazine.com

one Heart ♦ one Self ♦ one World

CPSIA information can be obtained at www.ICGtesting.com
Printed in the USA
LVOW10s0821230214

374728LV00008B/168/P

9 780988 833388